Praise for
Comfy Slippers and a Cup of Tea

"Julie has condensed a lifetime of studying and teaching personal development into this cozy little book. What is particularly lovely is that she writes just as if we are sitting in front of the fire—slippers on, tea in hand, sharing commonsense ideas about how to make life gentler, richer and more fulfilling. A gem."
Adrian Gilpin, author of *Unstoppable – The Pathway to Living An Inspired Life*

"A well-written, easy-to-understand and undeniably inspiring book on motivation and self-development. A must-read for everyone wanting to lead a happier and more fulfilled life."
Robin Barratt, writer, author and founder of the Bahrain Writers' Circle

"This easy-to-read book from Julie Lomas gives plenty of useful, straightforward guidance on everyday situations that can help any reader. It is pleasing to see a book offering holistic advice that anyone can make use of, regardless of their belief systems, philosophy or religion. We would happily recommend this book to members of our close family to help them in times of worry and stress."
Sue & Simon Lilly, authors on spirituality and various topics linked to holistic healing

"A delightful, enlightening book. Julie Lomas turns confused thinking around with her easy-to-read, powerful wisdom. She motivates you to instantly 'step into action.' This book is highly recommended for anyone who has ever doubted themselves."
Lucille Sheldon, psychotherapist

"What a wonderful book. Be prepared to be wrapped in Julie's gentle pure heart as you explore your own journey in the safety of your home through simple yet powerful tools. A must-read."
Mari Hall, author of *Reiki for the Soul, The Eleventh Doorway, Practical Reiki*, and *Reiki for Common Ailments.*

"What an inspiring book! It is easy-to-read and full of guidance for getting to know yourself and understand why you react in certain ways in situations. On top of that it includes tips and hints on how to start changing those negative encounters and thoughts, we all have, into positive ones. I believe this book should be read by teenagers, to give them a better understanding of life, so they realise that obstacles in life are common and that there are solutions."
Maggie Andersson, author of *Quintessential Woman*

COMFY SLIPPERS *and* A CUP OF TEA

COMMON SENSE AND WISDOM TO HELP GUIDE YOU TO A HAPPY LIFE

By Julie A Lomas

The Light Network

The Light Network

Published 2013 by Light Tree Books,
an imprint of The Light Network
www.thelightnetwork.com
ISBN: 978-0-9571596-6-2

Edited by Keidi Keating

Layout by Christi Koehl

Dedicated to Roy for his love, support, patience and my morning cup of tea.

Maitha, for inspiration, laughter and the many cups of tea we have shared.

To all my friends, family and teachers who have given me so much.

Contents

☕ x ☕

Foreword

Modern man, you and me, have acquired a great deal of knowledge and our heads are filled with it to the brim. The constant flow of this knowledge occupies so much space and time that we may have forgotten the Essential. In the fields of science and technology, man has taken a quantum leap in the past hundred years and a lot of it has become our common treasure. Many of us spend most of the day talking, thinking and dreaming of business geared towards survival and the accumulation of wealth. When carefully examined, however, what conceals itself as business may actually be fear. We think that we know how the Universe works and have "learned" not to question our social, cultural and religious conditioning. In the course of millennia we have worked out a social code of what is right or wrong, good and bad, desirable and what is to be discarded. Some of what we take as given may not be substantial and may in fact hinder our growth and restrict our freedom. With the computer age, information has picked up lightning speed. We know what is going on at any given time all over the Earth and we call all of this accumulated knowledge "living."

However, the most obvious and essential knowledge available to mankind has escaped our common attention almost entirely. We do not know who we are. And how can you expect someone to live a life of happiness and contentment and a life filled with love and celebration if he does not know himself? Our hearts are empty and most of us feel disconnected from our own true self, as well as from the Whole.

In the following pages Julie Lomas takes you on a journey to your Self. She lovingly leads you to become aware of your conditioning, of what you may erroneously think yourself to be. Your own belief systems and those of the people who "educated" you are questioned and discarded upon your own understanding. You are taught to funnel your past and present experiences through the filter of your innermost wisdom. Without judgement she assists you in identifying obstructive behavioural patterns and letting them go with love. Julie presents you with the paper and pen to write the story of your own life anew, the way you have dreamed about it, but lacked the courage until today.

Here and now, you are given simple yet powerful tools to aid you in your journey from being a leaf in the wind towards being a responsible (response-able) part of this wonderful playground here on Earth. With the help of a series of suggestions and questions you are gently guided towards discovering the unknown You.

And this is the art of self-discovery: you question and enquire; you succeed and fail; you lose and find yourself again and again, until one day you realise what you already knew when you were born. Julie's pure heart guides you towards this recognition with down to earth exercises and permanent encouragement, helping you to become conscious of the fact that you are exactly as you should be and that there is no need to become anyone but your Self.

~*Frank Arjava Petter, author*

Introduction

*"You are obligated to understand that you are unique in
the world. There has never been anyone like you because,
if there were, there would be no need for you to exist. You
are an utterly new thing in creation. Your life goal is to
realise this uniqueness."*
~Aaron Perlow

I welcome you all to this book, *Comfy Slippers and a Cup of
Tea*. I do not believe in coincidences, so if you are reading
this opening page it is obviously meant to be and for a short
time our energies are destined to meet. I do hope you stay
here longer and read the rest of this book. These pages are
filled with guidance, inner wisdom and plain common sense.
This book has been written in easy-to-read terms, with the
intention of helping you find more balance and happiness
in your life. It will also help you to drop the self-limiting,
outdated beliefs you may hold about yourself and lose some
of the emotional baggage we all carry around, which stops
us from enjoying the journey of our life.

Since 2004 I have been writing a newsletter focusing
on a different self-help topic each month. Since then the
mailing list for this has grown in number and also the
amount of countries it is sent to.

This book is based on a number of those newsletter
topics, after many of my readers, clients, friends and family
members suggested the idea of putting them together into
a book. Each month I receive many emails from people all

over the world saying things such as "I feel you wrote that newsletter for me." Over the years many people have written to me to say they are just going to "make a cup of tea, put their slippers on, put their feet up and read it," hence the title of the book.

In 2008 I participated in a Mind Body Spirit show in Dubai. I was stunned when people queued at our stand for up to two hours just to say hello and thank me for the positive down to earth advice on these monthly newsletters.

What finally made me start the process of putting the book together was when I was given an achievement award for my writing from a Humanitarian Group (IHM) in 2011 as 'Best Commentator on Human Life.' I was truly humbled by the award as I had never realised the impact these simple newsletters had on people's lives. I had and still have no idea how many readers I have or who is reading them, or where in the world. If this book helps just one person it is worth it. Since then I was awarded Best Peace Writer in 2013, also by IHM.

We all have access to that inner wisdom, which resides deep inside our spiritual heart. The key is to become more in-tune with it by taking care of not only our physical body, but also our mental, emotional and spiritual body, right up to our Higher Self or our Soul.

I hope this book begins to awaken some of that wisdom inside of you and that by reading the words, feeling the energy behind them and following the exercises, you too will begin to lead a happier and more fulfilled life.

It is my wish that we all awaken that inner wisdom and lead happier and more fulfilled lives. After all, we have all the answers we need deep inside. We just have to turn the key, open the door and perhaps also listen in the silence.

So make yourself a cup of tea, or coffee if you prefer, put your slippers on, your feet up and take some time for yourself. Now let your journey of inner discovery begin.

Wonderful Blessings and a happy life to you all

With Love,

Julie

Recommendations to help you make the most of this book

I recommend that you use a journal as a tool in your life. You may not wish to use it every day, in fact, you may only use it at certain times in your life, or when you are carrying out exercises. Your journal can turn into a place that provides valuable insight into yourself, your life and how you deal with issues. Over the months or years you may see patterns in your life that you had not seen or realised you had developed. Or perhaps you see issues that seem to arise over and over again.

When you buy your journal make sure it is beautiful or one that you feel excited about writing in. It should almost call you to write in it. However, some people may prefer an old scrap book or notebook and that is perfectly fine. Whatever suits you best and what you feel comfortable with.

Use your journal to make notes of how you feel. Write about things you want to change and write about all the wonderful things that happen.

There is no right way and no wrong way to use a journal. It is yours and it can become one of the most useful tools you ever have on the journey of your life. You can look back over the years and see how your life has changed, how you have moved on, how you used to think and feel and how you feel now.

It can help you to rediscover parts of yourself that you have forgotten, remember hidden talents or hobbies you once participated in and help you to gain clarity over situations and occurrences in your life.

Several of the exercises in this book suggest you write in your journal. But equally so, do not be put off at the thought of writing things down in a journal, as you can also use a sheet of plain paper if you wish.

Happy reading and enjoy your tea!

Your Energy and Vibration

"No one can deny or grant you anything. It all comes to you by virtue of your own vibration. If life is not going the way you want it to, stop complaining about it and either accept it or change it."
~Frank Arjava Petter

Everything that exists is energy! The world is energy, the Universe is energy, we are energy. And all energy interacts.

Whether or not you can see it, feel it, sense it or touch it, it is energy. From the thoughts that run through your mind, to the floor beneath your feet and the sky above your head, it all boils down to energy. Energy is never still. It pulsates and vibrates, constantly moving and changing.

For example, a floor is solid matter. You can see it, touch it and it supports your weight. It seems like it is just there, serving its purpose, but that does not mean it is still. The energy that makes up the floor is hard at work, vibrating at just the right speed and frequency to maintain its solid structure and physical appearance.

The thoughts which you hold in your mind are no less real than the floor beneath your feet, except they vibrate at a different speed and frequency. You may not be able to touch them, but that does not make them any less substantial. Your body has its own vibrations too. There is a whole lot going on underneath the skin that most of us do not even think about! Your body is denser energy than your thoughts. Energy follows thoughts and thoughts become things. Things are energy too.

Have you ever thought about the terminology you use to describe your moods? If you say you are feeling "low," people immediately conclude that you are troubled or depressed. However, a very positive experience may have you flying "high" for days.

Words such as high, low, rush, up and down can be used to portray not only how we are feeling, but also the vibes we are emitting; in other words our energy and vibration.

We all have good days and bad days. Our emotions often control us because we let them. Have you ever paid attention to how life tends to flow in relation to your mood? How about when you meet someone for the first time and immediately like or dislike them without fully understanding why? Everyone and everything throws off different energy vibrations. Sometimes we are consciously aware of the resonance, frequency and the intermingling vibrations that either harmonise or repel us. Because like attracts like, the vibes we emit are similar to a mating call, drawing in people, events and things that exist on the same or similar vibrational plane to our own.

Most of the time, looking good and feeling good go hand in hand. When we are feeling good about ourselves and our lives, we have more confidence and it shows. We are more charismatic and we appear brighter and more beautiful to ourselves and others. Those "happy to be alive" days are the best. We may dismiss them as luck or a fluke, but the reality is that on those days we have raised our vibration up a notch and as a result we experience an energetic boost.

On the other hand, when our vibrations drop down low, we usually feel tired, pessimistic and even depressed. Those vibrations are the energy we project and the energy we attract. This vibe is more likely to cause negative events to happen throughout our day. We tend to look at the incidents as the cause or source for our state of vibration, but often it is our vibrations that attract the incidents; the law of attraction.

Not all of us are meant to be one of those happy smiley people who seem to bounce around constantly with boundless energy, but each of us has a positive vibrational groove. We have all experienced that level of harmony before and with a little effort we can find it again and even increase it. When our mental and physical energies are in harmony, we buzz with personal power.

Life is not always easy; it can actually be very difficult at times, but there is no law that states we have to continually add to the chaos, confusion and suffering. With a little effort, we can all make our lives easier, happier, healthier and brighter. In turn, this will help to clear away some of our obstacles or attract what we need to surmount them.

If life is not going the way you want it to, change it. Put down that never-ending list of things to do and spend some time focusing on yourself. Understand that in your life, you are the point of origin, the place where everything begins and ends, therefore the vibrations you project are like a magnet drawing in things of the same frequency. When you truly understand that principle, you will feel a shift in consciousness and your vibrations will begin to change in accordance with that shift. Your life will change positively as you think more positively.

Words like "can't," "want" and "never" may begin to

fade, especially if your quest is truly and wholeheartedly geared toward happiness and improvement. These low frequency words are powerful in thought and it is human nature to believe the negative rather than the positive. These words are heavy and limiting and they hold down your vibration, the essence of you. Replace them with "will," "can" and "deserve" and that way you will create an opportunity rather than an obstacle. Believe those positive words and your vibration will increase and lighten and so will you.

Our perceptions not only influence but also create our realities. Like a ripple caused by throwing a pebble into water, the vibes we send out expand and touch others, in the same way as their vibes seek us. Some moments in life seem so perfect, but even though those moments pass, their vibrations can remain. Surround yourself with the people and things you love and which make you feel good and then you will consciously project love too.

Step Into Action

Changing your vibration is fairly easy, but maintaining that shift may take a little practice.

☕ Focus on the good things in your life, even when things are tough. Be grateful for all you have in your life, the good and the not so good.

☕ Visualise yourself as you want to be.

☕ Write down in your journal how you want your life to be and then imagine you are already living it.

☕ Meditate or sit quietly for five or ten minutes a day.

☕ Exercise. A short walk each day is enough.

☕ Recite positive affirmations that resonate with you.

☕ Absorb the energy of music that lifts you, revitalises

you, or brings you peace.

☕ Sing along to all your favourite records, or whatever songs you love to sing.

☕ Dance around the house, the garden or go dancing. Don't worry how you dance, just enjoy, let go and be happy.

☕ Laugh and surround yourself with people who make you laugh, watch TV shows that make you laugh, or laugh for no reason at all. Laughter is very good for you and your vibration.

These are just a few examples of things you can do to raise your frequency. With consistent and conscious effort, you will be able to measure your improvement and success.

Love yourself, you're worth it!

Awakening Spiritually

"The nature of rain is the same, but it makes thorns grow in the marshes and flowers in the gardens."
~Old Arab Proverb

If you have ever been in the presence of a deeply spiritual person, you might have felt a beautiful sense of peace and calm and you possibly wanted to stay in their company for as long as possible. This is because they have the gift of emitting spiritual love to everything and everyone around them. Spiritual love carries us into the silence of our original state of being. This silence contains the power to create harmony in all relationships and the sweetness to sustain them.

Different people define spirituality in different ways. Many confuse it for religion, thinking you have to be religious to be spiritual or vice versa. But that is not entirely true. Some of the most spiritual people I know have never visited a place of worship nor are they affiliated with any organised religious group. In my lifetime I have also met some so-called "religious" people who did not seem to be spiritual at all.

However, while the concepts of spirituality and religion are related, they are not inextricably linked. For example, a very religious person might simply accept doctrine, go to his/her chosen place of worship and never look within himself. Likewise, someone with no organised religion can spend a lifetime spreading love, compassion and kindness towards his fellowman, commune for hours in nature, give endlessly, be of service to people and endlessly ponder the organisation of the Universe.

Spirituality is not about attending Sunday Mass, reciting daily prayers or taking part in Friday Service (nor is it any specific religious practice, though that can be a part of it). Spirituality is about truly connecting with yourself, the world around you and your version of a higher power and the Universe. Spiritual people spread love and light wherever they go. People are drawn to them because of the peace and tranquillity that surround them. They exude warmth, compassion and light and they bring a beautiful energy to everyone they meet.

Most people are asleep, even though they are not aware of it. They live in the world they are presented with and they do not take the time to question what they see. If they do inquire about things, they often simply accept what they are told. However, the seeker, by definition, delves within for answers. The seeker learns that by awakening to the beauty of the world and living in the present, they create the world they want to live in, thus growing on all levels.

Although we all enter this world with no preconceptions or prejudgements, our physical and mental beings are bombarded by external and environmental conditioning. While much of our upbringing and belief systems are shaped by our families, teachers, media and society in general, we sometimes become too consumed and inhibited by these traditional values and roles and sometimes we hide behind them as it is easier than rocking the boat so to speak. In order to create an environment for positive spiritual development we must nurture our higher consciousness and inner self by deprogramming most of what we have been mentally taught. That does not mean straying from moral values and ethics, but changing our emotional limitations that lead to negativity, mental barriers and a narrow-minded way of thinking.

The difference between blind acceptance and true faith begins with exploration. We must go beyond science. It means accepting the metaphysical and realising there is so much more than what we physically see, such as psychics, astrology, universal energy and more. We create our own realities and those who are accurately tuned in, such as psychics, can even see those realities before they happen. We can too, if we learn to read the signs. It is the Universe's gift to those who pay attention.

To achieve spiritual growth, it is necessary to think and feel with an absolutely uninhibited mind and spirit. Deep within our core is a free spirit desperately wanting to break free from the mental fences we have built around ourselves in an effort to stay sheltered from harmful or painful situations. This free spirit is your real self, your "soul." And whether you choose to follow it or not, your soul wants to be released from your mental and emotional grip. It will always push you towards that whether you want it to or not. Sooner or later greater challenges will be thrown your way and you may feel as if your life is in turmoil. This is the soul's way of sending you the message that it wants to expand, grow and break free of self-imposed limitations. Your soul is "you."

The challenges will make you stop in your tracks and spring into action. Your soul speaks to you to give you the appropriate clues to achieve and maintain balance in all aspects of your life: mind, body and spirit. It wants you to grow spiritually so that you are ready to receive the blessings the Universe wants you to have. That includes living in complete balance, happiness and joy.

As the seasons and years come and go, we learn that by growing spiritually there is a new dawning of a deep and spiritual recognition and awareness of life, love and sense of purpose. Remember your "soul" is ready to be released from your everyday confines. All you must do is ask for spiritual guidance and the universal flow of energy will give your soul the power and tools to discover how you can truly enjoy your life destiny.

Step Into Action

To grow more spiritually aware means enhancing your life, your well-being and your happiness. It means being aware of what is around you and realising that you have a role to play. Everyone is unique and everyone has a place. The jigsaw of life would not be complete without you and your contribution.

☕ Each day really look around you and commune with nature in some way.

☕ Spirituality is everywhere you look if only you seek it. Each day notice the beauty of nature all around and see it all with open and loving eyes.

☕ Take time to breathe.

☕ Give gratitude for all the good things and even the not so good things in your life. Both contain valuable life lessons for us.

☕ Be grateful for all the people in your life, including the difficult ones.

☕ Look at everything as a lesson in learning. Thank those that cause you pain and those that give you pleasure.

☕ Look at the world through your heart.

☕ Love with all you have, trust with an open heart.

☕ Give all your attention to the task at hand and practice being in the moment.

☕ Live in the now, not tomorrow, for tomorrow never comes.

☕ Do not postpone your life, live it now for you do not know when your time on this planet will be over.

☕ Accept and do not judge others. Everyone has a unique path to follow and you have no right to judge another person if they are not doing what you want or think they should do.

Love yourself, you're worth it!

Overcoming Limiting Beliefs

*"An old belief is like an old shoe. We so value its comfort
that we fail to notice the hole in it."*

~Robert Brault

Many of us grow up believing things about ourselves that are simply not true and we tend to accept other people's beliefs and ideas as truth. This starts from when we are mere babies. Most of us are totally unaware that the majority of our sense of self is not only false and outdated, but the cause of everything we find difficult about our life.

Our beliefs are only a fraction of the real truth about life and our self. Almost all of what we believe to be true about ourselves, other people and the world is not true at all. Go back ten years and take a look at yourself then. Now ask yourself, is what you considered to be true then the same as what you consider to be true now? If not, how can you be sure that what you believe now is not another falsehood?

The experiences of your past, particularly those from childhood, no doubt caused you to adopt certain untrue belief systems about yourself and your capabilities. People in our past, such as parents, siblings and teachers tell us about our future and these become ingrained in our brains as memories. For example, they might say: "You're not the brightest person in the world, you're clumsy, you're not very athletic, your singing sounds like a frog, you're not exactly pretty, you're not the smartest kid in our family, you're too fat to be a model, you'll never be happy, you'll never be successful, people like us never do well in life, you're a terrible partner/spouse." The list is endless. These words are like a heavy weight which people carry around on their shoulders, in their hearts and minds, often for their entire life. When we are told something negative, it usually sinks in deeply and we believe it. Then, either consciously or subconsciously, we look for ways to corroborate it.

Sadly, people tend to believe the negative words rather than the positive ones. If someone tells you that you are brilliant at something or you look fantastic, it is much harder to believe or accept than if you are told you are ugly or rubbish at something. This has stemmed from centuries of conditioning.

These false beliefs about yourself and the world continue to drive negative patterns of thinking, feeling and behaving and they keep you trapped in a motionless state. That said, it is not your past that prevents you from being happy and successful, it is the fact you have bonded yourself to wounds sustained during that time. You cannot change the past, you can only change your reaction to it. The only moment of power you truly have is right now in the present.

The power of our beliefs can readily act as a filter through which we experience the external world. Our beliefs can actually grow their own legs and influence the way we see, feel and experience the events. They can be either potent or very limiting.

Our beliefs have become our human survival technique. When they are threatened we instinctively feel the need to defend them, as we literally "fight for our survival." Consequently, identifying and dismantling these beliefs can feel extremely frightening because a part of us does not believe we could survive without them! It has become a part of our so-called identity.

However, when we realise that we do not have to believe everything we think, we can choose to drop the heavy burden of someone else's beliefs and make our own decision about what we wish to believe. In this way we have the power to change our lives immediately.

When we begin to acknowledge and accept that our pain and suffering is the result of our negative thoughts and false beliefs we wake up to our thoughts and how they affect us. As a result, confidence in our value, self-worth and divinity grows and we begin to live free from the limiting shackles of our past beliefs.

We each have a rule book and a set of beliefs about what things mean and how things are. The key to success is taking control of our beliefs

Words are powerful no matter which way they are used. The old adage that "sticks and stones can break my bones but words can never hurt me" is not true. Words can be either the most powerful and destructive weapon or the most healing and liberating gift we bestow upon ourselves and others, so always take care of what you say to others, especially children.

Step Into Action

With this in mind, I challenge you to ask yourself the following questions and write the answers in your journal:
☕ Are you kind to yourself?
☕ If not why not?
☕Are you aware of the messages that you tell yourself

day in and day out?

☕Do you really believe the things you think about yourself? Look deep within yourself and do not be afraid to do so, you are just looking at the real you.

☕Where do these beliefs come from? Who told them to you?

☕Why do you continue to believe them? This is a hard one to deal with, but you can do it. The answers may shock you.

☕Are you striving to do and be your best? Think and be truthful with yourself.

☕Do you encourage and support others to be their best self and to do their best? Think hard and be truthful.

☕Next time you find yourself in a difficult situation ask yourself, "What do I believe about this situation that is causing me pain or difficulty?" Write it down.

☕Then ask yourself, "Is that thought true? Can I absolutely know it is true?" After you have answered yourself honestly, more than likely you will see that the thought is not true. So why do you let it continue?

I believe that we can all be our very best selves. We just have to TRUST and believe that we have the power to change. When we trust that change is possible, amazing things can and do happen. That is my belief. You do not have to make it one of yours but why not attempt it and see?

Love yourself, you're worth it.

Dealing with Anger

"For every minute you are angry, you lose sixty seconds of happiness."

~Anon

Do you ever get angry? Of course you do. We all do! It is one of the most natural human emotions. Sometimes it is healthy to get riled up, so long as it does not last too long! The energy of anger is powerful and it can be destructive if it is not contained.

Anger can ruin our peace of mind and damage important relationships. Its physical manifestations—faster breathing, racing pulse, hot rush of blood, adrenaline boost—all deplete our energy reserves placing stress on our hearts, nerves and respiratory functions. Ongoing anger can also be the cover for other emotions such as deep seated sadness, grief or confusion.

It is not a good idea to go around venting our anger on every person or thing that makes us mad. We cannot punch every person who we think has wronged us or smash car windows because someone parked in our parking spot.

Nevertheless, suppressed anger can prove almost as damaging as constantly venting our anger. Suppressed anger sooner or later causes illness in the body and maybe even the mind. Like every other emotion it needs to be expressed. On an energetic level anger often sits in the liver.

If channelled in the right direction, anger can help us to accomplish goals and push us to set our sights higher, even if we are just trying to prove someone wrong. Some of the world's greatest artists, poets and songwriters have used their anger to produce some of the most potent art and music ever. Leaders have transformed their anger to create social change.

It can also alert us when there is a problem that requires attention. It prompts us to defend ourselves or others when wronged. And it prevents us from passively accepting unjust situations.

Some might argue that anger is the flip side of love. It is a love and desire for truth that when channelled in the right direction can ultimately lead to doing the right thing. But to see these positive results, we must first learn how to constructively deal with our own anger, as well as the anger of others.

So what are some appropriate ways to honour yourself and deal with anger?

Acknowledge that you have an anger issue. Many angry people tend to blame the other person or institution without looking at themselves. They (or you) may say things like, "If only the driver hadn't cut me off, I wouldn't have punched him in the nose or rammed his car with mine," "If only he/she hadn't called me an idiot..," "If he/she hadn't lied to me.....let me down," and so on. Do not rationalise your actions in this way. Instead of seeing yourself as a victim, own the problem! It is not what happens to you but what you do with it that counts. Once you take responsibility, you can move on and understand your anger and yourself on a deeper level.

Decide what "need" has triggered your anger. Is it the need to be respected or a desire to be understood? Or is it about territory, which can be either physical or psychological?

Anger is often triggered when we feel disrespected or when our turf is encroached upon. People also use anger to cover up and deal with sadness and hurt. Once you have realised this, it can help clarify precisely what needs must be fulfilled.

When you become angry, or if you are feeling angry in general, you can ask yourself some simple questions such as:

☕ Am I using anger to disguise my true feelings? If so think about your true feelings and maybe write some of them down.

☕ In what way do I feel violated right now?

☕ Is it a lack of respect or a violation of territory that is making me angry?

☕ How would I change the situation if I could?

☕ What is my need at this moment?

☕ What would have to happen to make me feel that my needs for respect or territory are once again intact?

☕ What is my goal, not just for the moment, but in future interactions with this person or future occurrences of this situation?

☕ Do I feel hurt right now?

Ask yourself what this incident has triggered within you? Are you hiding something or denying something in terms of your life, beliefs, values or ideals that this situation or incident has brought to question?

Another way to look at your anger is to figure out what triggers it, the "hook" or your "hot button" so to speak.

Do you lose it when you are sitting in bumper-to-bumper traffic? When you face delays on public transportation? Sitting in airports waiting for delayed flights? In supermarket queues when the checkout girl seems to be taking forever or chatting to a colleague or the person in front of you is taking their time packing or paying and you are in a hurry? When you find out that your work colleague has screwed up an order yet again? When the bank has overcharged you? Or your insurance company refuse to pay for your claim as they say it is not covered? The list is endless.

Then there is incompetence. For instance, you wait 30 minutes on hold to get through to customer services, but then the assistant "accidentally" hangs up on you. Or you order a decaf coffee but when you cannot sleep that night you realise they gave you caffeinated. Or you learn that a certain airline has lost your baggage yet again! Or the travel agent has booked you the wrong flights and you are stranded in a foreign country.

Certain other situations can also trigger anger, such as when you know your friend/partner/acquaintance/work colleague is lying to you but you just cannot prove it, or you have been blatantly lied to and now the damage of that lie is causing you problems.

Once you have found your hooks, ask yourself things such as, "Have I encountered this particular hook before?" If the answer is yes, try to remember when, with whom and under what conditions. Ask yourself what happened when you encountered it in the past? Did you get really angry? Did any damaging or enduring consequences occur?

Love yourself, you're worth it.

Transforming Anger

"Anger is a tragic expression of unmet needs."
~Marshall Rosenberg Ph D.

The first of the five principles that Reiki Practitioners live by is "Ikaru Na," meaning "Don't be angry." That does not mean you should no longer get angry as sometimes anger is the only appropriate reaction. Anger may be good for you and it may also be good for the person it is directed to. Sometimes the other person may need to be shaken up and shaken out of his/her unconsciousness. Sometimes it is necessary for you to see that you are still as human and as neurotic as you ever were, therefore not misjudging your own state of mind, even though that might hurt. The word "ikaru" has an explosive character, but do not remain in that state of explosiveness. Anger might also be sadness in disguise. Instead of trying to manage the anger, look at the sadness in your heart. Acknowledge it, face it and feel it. Cry for the losses you have experienced, cry for loved ones you have lost without trying to make the pain go away and you will see your anger disappear all by itself.

Ideally, you should allow your anger to wash over you like a passing storm. This is easier said than done. Many people will blow their top off instead and suffer the consequences later.

Before you react it is better to take a few deep breaths and think things through. Be certain that you understand the circumstances not only from your own perspective, but from the other person's as well. Directly expressed anger generally makes a bad situation worse.

Do not put your anger on to someone else in any way, shape or form. This in itself can cause untold problems and the person on the receiving end will suffer for something he or she may have no knowledge about. No matter how rational that person is, the situation could get out of control because they will naturally tend to defend themselves.

So breathe deep and manage your anger rather than express it directly. When you are angry your judgement will be clouded. If possible, take a bath, go for a walk, watch a movie; do whatever it takes to remove yourself from the anger provoking situation.

If circumstances allow, why not write a letter in the heat of the moment then tear it up?

This technique will help you to collect your thoughts, sharpen your focus and hopefully express your rage in a harmless way. It may be that you are feeling angry with someone because they have triggered something inside you; something you are already angry about but are suppressing; something you know to be true but have not properly dealt with. The truth often hurts!

Avoid sending emails when you are angry. Any written communication is open to interpretation by the reader. When we write letters, we generally take care to think before we write. With emails, however, we often write and hit send before we really think, creating the potential for serious damage to relationships.

It will take a while for you to learn to adopt a new way of responding to anger and retooling the habits you have developed over a lifetime, so be easy on yourself. There will be times when you will lose it, but when that happens just take a step back and have a laugh then try again!

Step Into Action – suggestions to help transform anger

With these techniques you can work toward transforming anger into something positive:

☕ It is said that "the greatest remedy for anger is delay." Before doing or saying anything, try counting to ten or take a few deep breaths. This will give your body enough time to cool down from the adrenaline spike that comes with anger. If you can, wait a day before acting on an angry impulse.

☕ One might also say that the greatest remedy for anger is prevention. Recognise the stresses that lead to anger and deal with them before they develop.

☕ Take slow deep breaths to help calm your mind and body.

☕ Switching perspectives often helps. If possible think about the situation from the other side. This practice of empathy may help you to understand the situation better.

☕ Be honest and straightforward about your feelings, but communicate them in a non-hostile way. Instead of using accusations, stick to expressing your feelings.

☕ Dealing with angry people can be just as challenging as dealing with your own anger and sometimes you have to do both at the same time. In certain situations, dealing with an angry person can be fairly non-threatening. In other situations, your physical well-being could be at risk.

Suggested techniques to calm down an angry person:

To slow things down speak very slowly and softly (but not condescendingly) especially if the other person is yelling. This will help to calm down the other person at the same time as keeping you calm.

Let them say everything they want before trying to stop them or saying what you need to say first. Often this will calm the situation down quickly as they will vent off what they need to say and when they realise you are listening, their aggravation will lessen.

Ask questions and listen to the answers. Paraphrase the answers back to the person. This will let them know you are paying attention.

If an apology is requested, apologise even if you feel you did nothing wrong. An apology may help to calm the angry person down.

Acknowledge their anger, but do not validate it. Saying something like, "I can see you are angry" lets the other person know you understand their emotion.

Ask what you can do to make things better. If it is something you can do, do it.

You can talk about how the facts are perceived, but do not accuse the other person of being wrong. Keep your distance and refrain from touching the angry person, even if your impulse is to console.

Do not defend yourself. Just listen. A lot of really angry people just need to vent and feel like they have been heard.

Do not antagonise them further by arguing with them, or disagreeing with what they are saying at that time.

☕ Where possible try to keep eye contact with the angry person.

So the next time you are confronted with the ugly and powerful emotion of anger, stop and think how you can use some of these techniques to diffuse the situation.

Love yourself, you're worth it.

Dealing with Emotional Pain

"If an egg is broken by an outside force....life ends. If an egg breaks from within...life begins. Great things always happen from within."

~Anon

We all suffer pain throughout the course of our lives. Some people live in constant pain both emotionally and physically. I am sure that everyone who reads this has suffered from some sort of emotional pain.

Every day of our lives we are bombarded with quick fix, fast working remedies for pain, be it physical, emotional, mental or spiritual. In fact, these days there seems to be a pill available for everything. But do you ever think that a constant or regular pain is trying to tell us something important? Taking a pill only treats the symptom not the cause.

You may suffer from chronic headaches or head pain that you take pain relievers for regularly. Have you noticed that even pain reliever bottles tell you that if the symptoms persist you should see a doctor?

Rather than shutting out pain in the first place, consider an alternative approach for your pain, whether it is physical, mental, emotional or spiritual.

Make notes and familiarise yourself with the circumstances surrounding your discomfort and pain. Sit with it a while and see where it is coming from. If you endure constant headaches start to keep a note in your diary of when they happen. Does the pain usually start in a particular area? When does it appear? Is it related to any activities in your life or foods that you are eating? Does it start when you have spent time working under fluorescent lights, too long on the computer, or around certain people or places? Or is it triggered by stress? Once you are acquainted with the patterns and nature of your headache, you will have some ideas about how to address the cause, whether it is changing your eating patterns, removing yourself from stressful conditions or seeing a doctor to learn about migraines. I did this and started to notice different types of pain in different places and the different affects they had on my body. This uncovered another problem and I can now deal with it in a different way.

Use the same process with your emotional, mental and spiritual pain. It seems like a daunting step at first but it is not really. When we shut down, block out or pretend our pain does not exist, another problem shows up, especially with emotional pain. It does not actually go away because it is not being dealt with at the root cause! And emotional issues eventually become physical in some way and then the issue grows even harder to deal with. Emotional and mental pain is serious. It is ok to hurt, it is ok to sit with it for a while, but it is not ok if you constantly shut it out and fail to deal with it.

Imagine or picture your mind and your inner being as a large house with lots of closets or cupboards. Notice that these closets and cupboards are full of accumulated, rotting junk where you have hidden and stored all the unresolved emotional and mental pain of your entire life, including everything hurtful you have been told since childhood. When you were told to stop whining, stop crying, turn out the lights, that you are stupid, that you do not have a brain, that you will never amount to much, that you need to grow up. These closets and cupboards are often so crammed that if you open the door the contents will fall out on top of you in great piles; old grudges, childhood terrors, betrayals, disappointments and much more.

It is essential that you de-clutter these emotional closets because what is stored in them affects every day of your life, including how you respond to the world and what you expect out of life. Clearing out the closets will help you to come to terms with your emotional and mental pain and as a result free a huge amount of energy, enabling you to enjoy life more.

So open the doors to let the ghosts out and then start to get acquainted with them one by one. Get to know and understand the source of your sadness, pessimism, phobias and fears. Use meditation, journaling or any of the countless other self-help techniques available these days and you are likely to learn some surprising things!

Perhaps you know you are in pain because you broke up with your partner/lover/spouse. That is so obvious, you think, so what is there to learn? Failed relationships are a universally accepted reason for emotional pain, but there still may be lessons to learn, especially if this pain is a constant cycle in your relationships.

Ask yourself if you were happy in the relationship. Maybe you realise you were not and had been thinking of moving on. In this case, the emotional pain may be present because you are worried about being embarrassed in front of your friends. Or maybe you feel like a failure. Or you are annoyed and angry that your parents were right when they said your partner was a loser. When you look at it in this analytical and truthful way the light bulb flickers on and you realise a part of you believes the breakup means you are unlovable, that you will never find happiness in a relationship, that you are a loser. Once you have got to the core of the issue, the real journey begins. You can get to "know your pain" and follow its path to wisdom and healing.

When you are dealing with deep-seated stuff from your past, it is very important to look at it from the viewpoint of who you are today. That alone can bring about a tremendous shift! It is also important to recognise when you may need help and another viewpoint, whether from a life coach, a counsellor, a close friend or a self-help book which deals with your challenges.

It is also important to remember that this is not about getting rid of pain. It is about letting the pain show you how to honour yourself and your needs, about learning from the wisdom hidden in the corners of your mind and soul and clearing the rubble from your path, allowing for a happier, more positive future with far less pain and far more love and peace.

The next time pain shows up in your life welcome it as a teacher and motivator rather than just a pain! And remember to use it to de-clutter your internal closets.

Step Into Action

☕ In your journal write down the pain you are feeling, whether physical or emotional.

☕ If it is physical sit with it for a while and see/hear or

feel what the pain tells you. Where is it coming from? Make notes on when it happens, where or why. Is it situation related? Does it only happen on certain days?

☕ Do the same with emotional and mental pain and then look at each situation and see what patterns arise. Open the closets in your mind and let each ghost out one by one.

☕ Get help if you need it. There is nothing wrong with asking for help, we all need it at different points in our lives.

☕ Talk it through with a trusted friend or qualified therapist. Consider seeing a life coach/therapist/counsellor.

☕ Read some of the excellent self-help books that are available.

☕ Meditate on the situation, sitting with the real you.

☕ Attend one of my workshops or someone else's workshops on healing the self.

☕ Do not be afraid to deal with it now. The sooner you do, the sooner you will lead a pain free, happier life.

Love yourself, you're worth it.

Dealing with
Verbal Abuse

"All cruelty springs from weakness."

~Anon

We have all been on the receiving end of verbal attacks, which often hurt more than physical attacks. The verbal attack may come from anywhere and anyone, including parents, siblings, teachers, relations, friends, workmates, your boss or the people you interact with in the outside world. Often there is no apparent reason. These days the world seems to be full of angry people who attack each other verbally. Such an incident has the potential to ruin your day in an instant. It can send you quivering into a corner, knock your confidence, leave you in a state of disbelief, breakdown into tears or make you angry, reactive and aggressive, draining all your energy. It is wise to remember that a verbal attack is all about them and nothing about you!

When people are angry or attacking others verbally, it is usually because they are angry inside, unhappy or frustrated and they vent because they can. It is far easier for them to vent at others than deal with their own personal issues. And if you are honest with yourself, I am sure that at some point you have vented at others in the same way.

However, whether the verbal ambush comes from someone who is plagued with jealousy, someone who has an inferiority complex or someone who is just plain rude and angry, you owe it to yourself not to internalise the attack. When you internalise it you become eaten up with anguish and the other person's anger and pain. They may be suffering from emotional or mental pain and confusion, but there is no reason for you to suffer it too. This is easier said than done because words are very powerful and they affect us deeply.

When you are faced with a verbally abusive person it is important to centre your emotions and your confidence. Remember, a predator or a bully is always searching for prey, as that is what they do best. If you reveal a low self-esteem or fear the bully will be tempted to attack that weakness. So breathe deeply, relax then take a moment to strengthen your mental and emotional gates by boosting your self-confidence. Focus on your strengths and the respect and love you have for yourself. That way the verbal attacks will fail to breech those iron strong mental and emotional defences, preventing you from having a more serious emotional injury. You will discover an emotional balance this way. It takes practice but you can do it!

Keep in mind that the verbal attacker is only venting their anger and pain to get a reaction from you or people around you. By reminding yourself of that, when a verbal assault begins you will feel more confident and impervious to the verbal rocks hurled in your direction. The attacker needs you to react in order to feed their outburst, so why give them what they want? By not reacting you starve the attacker of fuel and therefore you gain control over the interaction.

Another way to neutralise the situation is to call them out on their bullying and rudeness. This can be hard to do, but if you are able to muster the courage and confidence it works. A calm and confidently delivered phrase, such as "That's really rude and you need to back off," or "There's no need to be so mean" shows them that you are willing to stand up for yourself. It also displays your unwillingness to be their verbal punching bag. If possible, even if you are shaking in your shoes, say these words with a smile, as a smile is very disarming. Even look the other person directly in the eyes if possible.

You can also change the direction of the attack, which throws the attacker off-balance. Bullies do not like their own medicine and when confronted they usually crumble in some way. The bully will expect a fight-or-flight-type response after a verbal outrage, not a skilful or confident navigator who grabs those conversational reigns right out of their hands. For example, if someone attacks you about a mistake you may have made in the past, a confident person might say, "Look how well things turned out for me though." Or, "You can't change the past, what was done was done, it is now time to move on, Let go!" A calm, simple and non-aggressive response literally disarms them. Try not to bite or take up their angry stance. Instead, stay calm, smile and say no more than necessary. Be the better person and let them use up their anger on themselves. In time they will burn themselves out and calm down. Refraining from engaging in a verbal attack or abuse is the best method of response and if you are able to disengage your emotions from their opinion then even better.

There is no better self-defence than not caring what the other person thinks or says. If you do not play the victim and do not sink to their level, it is likely that they will feel a sense of shame in front of their peers or co-workers and realise they are only harming themselves. At some point they will implode.

If the person who is verbally abusing you is a friend, or even your spouse and it is a continuous part of your relationship with them, maybe it is time to question your relationship and where possible, distance yourself from them. Do not put yourself in the path of verbal abuse if you can avoid it.

A wonderful old age adage good to remember in situations like these is, "All cruelty springs from weakness" and that is so very true. Bullies are usually sad, angry, weak people who enjoy hurting others because it is themselves who hurt inside. They have a need to be pitied and they are the victims of their own self-loathing. As I said at the beginning, it is all about them, not about you.

Step Into Action

☕ In your journal write down the names of people who verbally attack you and how it makes you feel.

☕ Think carefully about possible calm responses to disarm them.

☕ Remember, if you do not fuel their attack it will quickly run out of energy.

☕ Remember, you are not a victim and you can change anything you wish in your life.

☕ Remove yourself from the company of people who are verbally offensive where possible. There is no reason to remain in their company.

☕ Build your confidence and inner peace by taking time out for a few minutes each day to meditate. This in itself will bring you to a more peaceful place within.

☕ Visualise yourself protected from verbal attack by

a mirror that sends the attacker's words, venom and energy back to them without affecting you in any way.

Love yourself, you're worth it.

Dealing with Loneliness

"The most terrible poverty is loneliness."
~Mother Teresa

In the immortal words of the song Eleanor Rigby, the depth of loneliness and sadness is brought home to us.

Eleanor Rigby picks up the rice in the church where a wedding has been.
Lives in a dream.
Waits at the window, wearing the face that she keeps in a jar by the door.
Who is it for?

Eleanor Rigby died in the church and was buried along with her name.
Nobody came.

All the lonely people—where do they all come from?
All the lonely people—where do they all belong?

Loneliness is one of the most heartrending conditions we experience. It leaves us feeling hopeless, desperate, abandoned and that the world and God has forgotten us or does not care about us.

Whether the loneliness we are experiencing follows the death of a loved one or the end of a relationship, a situation change, a job loss or for no apparent reason, we all have times when we feel lonely or abandoned and we have a need to reconnect.

Sometimes, it can creep up on us, unexpected in its intensity, maybe even when we are in a room full of people, on a train, at a concert, anywhere. Loneliness is a very common human emotion.

After a significant loss, like a death or the end of a long-term relationship, it is good to take time to heal and to treat yourself with all the kindness you would muster for a child who has lost a parent. Do not hide how you feel from those who love you.

Let people in, even if you feel like shutting down. Try to stay healthy; go for walks, eat nutritious food and get plenty of sleep. Every day remind yourself to keep breathing and keep moving. Make use of whatever spiritual tradition gives you comfort. Do things that generally make you happy.

For short-term or new loneliness, it is important that you feel your pain. No matter how terrible it feels, do not try to hide from it or run away. What makes this tough is that you cannot shut down either, you have got to keep on living your life, even if it feels like you are just going through the motions. Grief comes in waves (which will gradually become fewer and farther in-between), so when you happen to notice something like the beauty of the morning, drink that in as a moment of grace and know that you are starting to come through your pain.

This does not work with chronic long-term loneliness, as the pain will be all consuming. In such cases, the sufferer may reach a stage where they do not know how to live without the loneliness; it becomes a part of their personality, a way to survive. These people need something deeper such as a spiritual belief or system or someone to give them time.

The interesting thing about chronic loneliness is that people often impose it upon themselves. Lonely people are often their own worst enemies because they retreat from social contact when their unrealistic expectations of relationships do not meet the standards they set or sometimes because they have been badly hurt or abused in childhood. People may also become alienated by expecting or demanding too much of those around them. Lonely people often suffer from a distorted logic and hold on to thoughts such as:

"I am alone, therefore no one wants to be with me. If no one wants to be with me, how can I escape from my loneliness? If they won't help me I will reject them too."

So it becomes a vicious cycle, which brings more negative thinking, reinforces false beliefs and makes the situation worse by causing the person concerned to shun the very thing they crave the most: other people.

Lonely people often set themselves up for failure by sabotaging opportunities to make friends and acquaintances. They are often described as living on the periphery of life, as if watching from the outside of a fish bowl, wishing that somehow they could be inside.

Of course we are all different and there are some people who choose to be alone for the simple reason that they feel life has nothing to offer them or because they trust only themselves. There are others who simply enjoy being on their own. We, as a society, may think they are lonely when they are not and we must honour and respect their wish to be left alone. People who want to be alone are usually not lonely.

For the new lonely, there are few things as disconcerting or alienating as being surrounded by a circle of laughing people while you sit alone, watching. Nevertheless, meeting new people can be daunting, especially when they are a tight group and you feel like an unwanted outsider or intruder.

Starting a new job, transferring to a new school or moving to a new city can all offer new lessons in loneliness. While this will all change as soon as you meet like-minded people, sometimes when people are painfully shy, nervous or unable to meet new friends, it can seem to take forever and that is when loneliness sets in.

If allowed to develop unchecked, this loneliness becomes depression and when depression takes over, everything in life becomes hard work, creating a situation which feels like it is impossible to come out of. Loneliness and depression often go hand in hand. Unfortunately, in situations such as this, the depression is diagnosed and treated and while the feeling of loneliness that accompanies it goes away the prescribed drugs numb the emotions. However, when people are treated for depression when the root cause is actually loneliness, the treatment only holds the symptoms at bay without curing the problem. It is a fine line.

A new environment demands unfamiliar effort. In your hometown or your last job, it seemed as if you just had friends, but now you need to put yourself in situations where you can make them. Explore your interests by going to classes you enjoy. Maybe join a book club or go to book signings, art galleries, museums, if you like sports sign up for sports teams or join a yoga group. By doing things like this you will meet people you share an interest with, increasing the odds of finding someone to befriend. Put yourself out there for a while and you will start to run into people you can connect with.

If you have ongoing loneliness and feel utterly alone, isolated and empty or you are experiencing deep disconnection to your life, first ask yourself:

"Am I ignoring something that my soul wants to be acknowledged for? Is there a dream or a goal being repressed or denied?"

Are you keeping a secret that separates you from those you love? Or are you simply in a circle of people with whom you have little in common? Often this type of loneliness demands working with a professional to uncover its core and to find a way out.

Whatever the cause, know that you are not alone. Even if you feel like no one is close to you, it is important to remember that loneliness, grief, loss and occasional disconnection are all part of the human condition. With time, effort and guidance, you will find yourself feeling more connected and back to your usual self.

Loneliness can really limit our ability to be a part of fulfilling opportunities and relationships. Take the bold step to reach outside of yourself and you will be surprised to find what you have been missing. There are many groups and associations out there who can help.

Step Into Action – counteracting loneliness

☕ If it is too difficult to be with people for the sake of socialising take a course, join a craft class, join a book club, gym, parent group or take up a new hobby that involves group participation.

☕ If suitable join a spiritual group of your own choosing.

☕ Do some serious reality checking about what you expect of others and yourself. A therapy such as life coaching or counselling is a good way to get the feedback you need.

☕ Consider helping out in a charity group/animal rescue centre or a place where the people are community centred rather than self-centred.

☕ Reach out to others and you will be surprised at how responsive they will be. Getting involved in volunteer work is an excellent and non-threatening place to begin.

☕ If shyness is a problem, join an organisation such as Toastmasters.

☕ Take a training course for assertiveness that caters specifically to these kinds of concerns.

Love yourself, you're worth it.

Dealing with Worry

"Blessed is the person who is too busy to worry in the daytime and too sleepy to worry at night."

~Anon

For many, Reiki is the entry point onto a more spiritual path. Reiki involves using universal energy to heal yourself and others. However, it is also about how you live your life.

I myself am a Reiki Practitioner. Central to our Reiki beliefs are five simple principles that, when applied on a daily basis, can have a profound positive impact on our life. One of these principles is 'Just for today do not worry,' or "Shinpai Suna." This is an easy thing to say but perhaps not such an easy thing to do. Or is it?

Worrying is a common daily activity, perhaps the greatest misuse of our mental energy and a complete waste of time. It can even kill you. Worry is one of the most toxic substances, for body, mind and soul, along with fear and guilt. They often act like siblings and appear together, making your life difficult!

We each have an average of 50,000 to 60,000 thoughts a day and the majority of them are negative. They are worries. They do not tend to be seriously dark, such as running rampage with a machine gun, but simple little niggles like, "Did I lock the door? Where are my keys? Am I going to be late?" According to researchers, most of us spend about one hour and 46 minutes a day worrying—that is five years and two months of our lifetime. Compared to men, women spend an extra five weeks of their lives worrying. The number one worry is money, followed by health and then relationships.

We worry about things that have happened in the past. We worry about things that might happen in the future. Ultimately, there is a common thread to our worries—they are all based on fiction. We think about the past and worry about potential future consequences. We imagine that the past will come back to haunt us. We have no real evidence that it will, but we allow our creativity to rearrange the facts into an imaginary tale of woe. The only place where these outcomes are real is in our imagination.

We take current situations and allow our imagination to project them into potential future scenarios, persuading ourselves to believe these outcomes are real. Again, the only place they are real is in our imagination.

There is no doubt that the mind is a remarkable instrument. It is able to recall countless past memories and picture infinite possible future events. With such abilities, it can take advantage of everything you have learned to help you adapt to the world. Your creativity and imagination know no bounds and with a positive outlook on life anything is possible. Unfortunately, however, even the most positive thinkers have moments of doubt, when the odd negative thought creeps in and creates worries. For many of us, a potential problem is far bigger than positive outcomes so we allow worry to dominate our lives.

We think about depressing past events, which caused us anxiety. We think about a whole range of negative future events that might happen and how bad they will make us feel. Sometimes, for no apparent reason, we simply cannot stop thinking about such things. But each time we think about them, our body reacts as if the event were actually happening. This can make us quite sick, both emotionally and physically. This is the incredible power of the mind. Despite the fact that most people acknowledge worry as a waste of time and energy, it is still one of the most common lessons we learn from our parents. The prevailing myth handed down from generation to generation is, "It's good to worry as it shows you care." This, of course, is nonsense!

Worry is fear. Care is love. Fear and love are polar opposites. If you stop for a moment and become aware of why you are worrying about someone else you may find it is motivated by selfishness. Really you are worried for yourself. You are worried about how you will feel if something bad happens to someone else.

You do not solve problems by thinking; you create problems by thinking. Worry thinking is simply a learned habit, an addiction that is fed by a toxic diet of bad news, unfortunate events and the personal traumas of others.

Don't Worry Be Happy was the title of a hit song a few years ago. However, for many people not worrying is not easy, as worry has become a mental or emotional drug and just saying "be happy" is a threat to that drug. Besides, many people think they are quite happy worrying! In fact, some people only get really worried when they think they have nothing to worry about!

"If Only" Thoughts

"If only" refers to thoughts about an unhappy event that you wish had not happened. The event has left you with an unresolved emotional feeling and under these circumstances your mind continues to attempt to resolve it, figure out what went wrong and how to fix it.

Unfortunately, because the event has already happened, nothing can be done. You cannot go back in time and miraculously have the event turn out differently. But when your mind recalls the event, its natural tendency is to continue attempting to solve the problem with a more acceptable outcome.

"What If" Thoughts

"What if" refers to thoughts about the future. In the case of worry, these thoughts are about any number of possible disagreeable or unpleasant things that could happen:

"What if I have a car accident?"

"What if I run out of money and can't pay my bills?"

"What if my partner no longer loves me?"

"What if I make a mistake and everyone thinks I'm a fool because of it?"

"What if my children fail their exams?"

Each of these is a possible future event, but only a possible one. If you think about it enough you will make yourself depressed or anxious, no matter how unlikely it is that such an event will actually happen. You could even manifest it. Moreover, for every negative event, there is a positive event that is just as likely to happen:

"What if I don't have a car accident and arrive safe and sound?"

"What if I don't run out of money and can pay all my bills?"

"What if my partner loves me more each day?"

"What if I make a great discovery and everyone thinks I'm a genius?"

"What if the children pass their exams with flying colours?"

If we really think about it, there are an infinite number of potential outcomes along our path. Can we really worry about them all?

As mentioned at the beginning of this chapter, Reiki is about energy and when we look more closely at the principles we see that they are all about energy too. Suggesting we do not worry is really suggesting that we do not waste energy on things we have no influence over.

Most of our worries centre around things that have already happened and things that have not yet happened (but might). In truth the things that have already happened are behind us. We cannot change the past so there is no point wasting our energy worrying about it. If we have forgotten our keys, we have forgotten our keys. We cannot "unforget" our keys. However, once we accept that we do not have our keys, we can put positive energy into a plan of action that might make the situation easier, calling a locksmith or a friend who has a spare key, for example.

Similarly, when we worry about problems that "might" arise in the future, we also waste energy because there is a good chance that the problem will never arise. If we were to channel energy into every possible future outcome, we would simply wear ourselves into the ground. It is a much better idea to put your energy into positive future outcomes and make them happen. You are what you manifest, so make sure you manifest positive events rather than worrying about the possible negatives.

Reiki Guru Frank Arjava Petter has the following to say about worry:

"You are not at the mercy of worry. If you understand that no worry is personal, it is a collective dis-ease. If a worry is not 'your own' maybe the next time it comes to you, you can look at it from the outside. Look at it as if it does not belong to you personally and you will see that you do suddenly have a choice; either you energise the worry with your active participation, or you don't. If you don't participate in it, you see it and you let it go. Eventually the worry runs out of gas and, after continuing from the past momentum for a little while, it comes to a full stop. And if no gas station is in sight, the worry will starve to death until the next worry comes to you. The same dynamic is applicable for thought. Watch it and it will eventually go away... Not worrying does not necessarily make all your challenges go away, but you will be able to deal with them more effectively, with less suffering and more joy. Then life may just be fun. Oops!"

Step Into Action

To begin letting go of your worries, at the end of each day write a simple list of all the things you worried about. You can do this in your journal or on a piece of paper, there is no right or wrong way. Next to each item write down what you will actually do about it.

Ask yourself the question: What percentage of your thoughts were worry thoughts and what percentage actually happened?

Reflect: "Don't Worry Be Happy"—make notes in your journal or notebook on the difference between worry and happy.

☕ Remember: You do not solve problems by thinking, you actually create problems by thinking. The solution always appears when you step out of thinking and become still and present, even if only for a moment. Try to let go of excessive thinking and see how everything changes.

☕ Read the book *The Power of Now* by Eckhart Tolle—be here in the "Now."

☕ Remember the Reiki principal, 'Just for today do not worry.' Or even learn Reiki.

☕ Give your worries to the Universe. Write down everything you are worrying about then literally give it to the Universe as if you are posting a letter. Just writing them down will take away some of the worry in itself, especially when you see how insignificant and far-fetched some of them are.

☕ Programme a clear quartz crystal to help you stop worrying.

Towards the end of his life, Winston Churchill said: "When I look back on all the words I have read, I remember the story of the man who said on his death bed that he'd had a lot of trouble in his life that never happened."

Do not let this be you. Release your worries and move forward.

Love yourself, you're worth it.

Getting to the Bottom of Denial

"The thing about denial is that it doesn't feel like denial when it's going on."

~Georgina Kleege

Denial is the refusal to acknowledge the existence or severity of unpleasant external realities or internal thoughts and feelings. At some time in our lives we have all lived in a state of denial.

Denial can be thought of as a complex psychological process where there may be some conscious knowledge or awareness of events in the world, but somehow one fails to feel their emotional impact or see their logical consequences. It is an attempt to reject unacceptable feelings, needs, thoughts, wishes or even a painful external reality that alters the perception of ourselves. This psychological defence mechanism temporarily protects us from:

☕ Knowledge—things we do not want to know.

☕ Insight or awareness that threatens our self-esteem, our mental or physical health or our security (things we do not want to think about).

☕ Unacceptable feelings we do not want to feel.

Every one of us has had to face an unpleasant reality or painful truth throughout our lives and at the very least we desperately wished it would go away. The first words which leave the mouth of someone notified about the sudden death of a friend or loved one is usually the involuntary exclamation of, "NO!" This angry refusal to accept the pain we would feel if the death were real is perfectly natural. The negative reaction gives us time to readjust our thinking and our feelings and prepare mentally and physically for the reality of death.

But if you are still saying, "No, it can't be true!" days and weeks after the death, refusing to face the reality, you are in serious denial and this will cause you and those around you additional problems. This is not a healthy place to be.

One situation where the concept of psychological denial is used quite frequently is in the chemical dependency field (drug and alcohol abuse). Anyone who has dealt with an addict has probably heard one of the following phrases or something similar:

"I could quit anytime I wanted."	False
"I'd quit if people would leave me alone."	False. They are using other people as an excuse not to deal with the issue.
"I can handle it on my own."	False. People in denial usually need outside help, especially addicts.
"I'm under stress and it helps me to relax."	False. It can make the problem much worse.

Denial is also commonly used by people with chronic illnesses or terminal illness such as diabetes, saying things such as: "I can eat anything I want;" people with heart problems—"I'm not really having chest pain I am just a bit out of breath;" Cancer—"It's just a small cough, or it's not really a lump I must have just knocked myself;" or AIDS— "I'm not gay or a drug user so I couldn't get it." The list is endless. When confronted, they become angry and usually contend that it is their confronter who has the problem, not them.

The world of denial allows someone to believe something is true, when it is obvious to everyone else that it is false. It permits someone to pretend they are feeling love or some other emotion when they are actually behaving in an awful manner. It hides the truth by using big words and grand concepts to prevent an individual from feeling unacceptable feelings.

Denial can make otherwise intelligent individuals behave in an irrational manner because they are too threatened by the truth and unable to process what is perfectly apparent to everyone. People who live in denial go through their daily lives secure in the knowledge that their self-image is protected against any information, feelings or awareness that might make them have to change their view of the world. Nothing, not facts, not observable behaviour, not the use of reason, logic or their own senses will make someone in denial re-evaluate that world view.

Denial is a way of retaining sanity when experiencing unbearable pain and a way to avoid the risk of change as a result of problems or loss. People in denial can seem unemotional, apathetic or indifferent in the face of loss or facing terminal illness. They may be childlike, dependent on others to reassure them that everything will be all right. They seem to be running away from the truth or they avoid or reject those intent on confronting them about their problems.

So how can we cope with this denial in others? A great deal of patience is needed in order to allow them time to confront their loss or problems. We need to be careful how we confront them, so they do not run away or withdraw from reality even more. We need to be ready for their resistance in dealing with the truth about their loss and problems, but at the same time offer them our support and understanding and be ready with a rational perspective to help them to refute their current irrational beliefs. It is important to resist solving their problems for them. If possible provide them with subtle means to face the problem by giving them magazine or newspaper articles, pamphlets or books on the subject; suggesting TV and radio programs or proposing professional help.

So what about ourselves? We all deny things about ourselves, our lives and our emotions. How can we confront denial in our own life? Try this simple action plan to discover if you are in denial and what you might be able to do to change the situation.

Step Into Action

Use your journal or a notebook for this part. Take your time and most importantly be honest with yourself. Stand in your truth.

☕ Think about your life. Think about the highs and lows, the good and the bad. Are there any areas you may be indenial about? Write them all down.

☕ Have you recently faced any problems or upsets that you do not want to talk about? Again be honest with yourself, even if they are just minor things that have bothered you.

☕Can you recall people trying to move you beyond a blockage recently, perhaps saying things like:

☕ You really need to let go of this pain now.

☕ It is time to move on.

☕ You seem to be eating/drinking/smoking a lot more than usual these days.

☕ You don't seem yourself—is everything ok?

If you come to the conclusion that there is something in your life you are in denial about then start by asking yourself honestly why you are in denial.

☕Ask yourself what the benefits are to be gained by your denial.

☕Ask yourself what is too painful to face and why.

☕Learn to recognise when you are caught up in magical or fantasy thinking about your problem or loss and then recognise the negative consequences that result from your denial behaviour.

☕Do your best not to allow yourself to fall back into a safe emotional zone, but to keep your emotional response open and honest.

☕Learn to recognise when you are hiding behind a "nice" mask when discussing your loss or problems. Allow yourself to express negative or embarrassing emotions as you confront your problems. For example, crying, feeling lost, feeling confused or scared.

☕Allow yourself to admit to being out of control and try trusting others to help you with your problem. It is important to admit our vulnerability and our need for assistance. It is human to have problems and to experience loss; it is not a sign of a lack of value or being a failure.

♨Ask others to not allow you to deny or avoid the truth about your loss or problems. Denial is a natural stage in the loss/grief response and we need to maintain our sense of perspective, allowing ourselves to go through the problems as a growth experience.

♨If you are really struggling and you know you need help, then get the help you need. Ask your doctor or therapist to recommend a programme or counselling. Help is always at hand and there is nothing to be ashamed about in asking for it.

Love yourself, you're worth it.

Feeling Sad

"You cannot protect yourself from sadness without protecting yourself from happiness."
~Jonathan Safran Foer

Are you feeling down? If so, you are not alone as everyone feels sad from time to time. It is highly likely that the things bugging you have affected billions of other people too. Instead of fighting the feelings it is a good idea to go with the flow and know that this too will pass. And once it does you will be a whole lot stronger.

Some people experience sad feelings on occasion while others have them fairly often. When you are in a sad mood, it may feel like it will last forever, but usually these feelings do not last for long, a few hours, a day or two, maybe longer after the loss of someone close. A deeper, more intense sadness that lasts a lot longer is called depression.

Sadness is like the dark side. For many, it is a state of mind. Everything in your world is painful. You are sad, alone and stuck in the throes of despair. What makes this worse is when everyone around you is smiling and happy, completely unaffected by the suffocating force bringing you down.

Doctors hand out anti-depressants like sweets, world famous speakers tell you that you too can be happy and the shelves of bookstores are littered with self-help books, such as *The Secret*.

The Secret can be found in practically every book store or new age store. It is regularly mentioned on popular talk shows and to be fair, it is helping millions of people, telling us we can have whatever we want in life. But it also imparts the message that we have to be happy and positive all the time. Like attracts like so if you are sad you will only attract more sadness. It is not uncommon to then feel as if you are doing something wrong, thinking you will never achieve happiness if you carry on feeling sad. As a result you beat yourself up even more and feel even sadder!

Then there is the media and Hollywood and the Hallmark channel, all which advertise notions of fairy tale endings, beautiful stories, happy people. The protagonists always end up together and that is what we want to see because deep down we wish that would happen in our own lives. Then when they find each other the movie ends and the subsequent ups and downs are not shown. When you are absorbed in the fantasy world, remember that is what it is and move on

There are times in life when you just cannot be happy so allow the feelings. It is ok to be sad! It is normal to sometimes feel sad.

Sadness, loneliness and despair are all part of the human condition. But for some strange reason there is a new epidemic where people seem to think they need to be happy all the time. They think sadness is wrong and there is something wrong with them for feeling sad. But that is not the case!

If you feel sad occasionally, maybe it is time to say to some of the famous speakers, "I am sad. I am sad and I am going to wallow in it, at least for a few days! It's ok to be sad sometimes!"

I am certainly not saying to let sadness rule your life, but do not rule it out either! If you do not sort through the feelings of pain, they will linger and they may even get worse.

What is Sadness?

Sadness is one of the many, normal human emotions or moods that we all have. It is the emotion people feel when they have lost something important, when they have been disappointed about something or when something sad has happened to them or to someone else they know. When they are lonely, people often feel sad. When you are sad, the world may seem dark and unfriendly. You might feel like you have nothing to look forward to. Sadness makes you feel like crying and sometimes the tears are hard to stop. Crying often makes you feel better, but not always. Sometimes when you feel sad, you just want to be left alone for a little while. Or you might want someone to comfort you or keep you company while you go through the sad feeling. Talking or even writing down what has made you sad usually helps the feeling to leave.

When sadness starts to go away it can feel like a heavy blanket is being lifted from your shoulders.

Feeling sad every once in a while is perfectly natural. Maybe you did not get something you really wanted. Maybe you miss somebody deeply. Maybe somebody you really like does not want to be friends and you do not feel so great about yourself. Maybe an illness or condition gets in the way of doing the things you want to do. There are lots of reasons why people feel sadness. Most of the time, sadness is because of a loss or separation, a difficult change, disappointment about something or relationship problems. Loss and separation are the most common cause of sadness.

It is a very sad thing to lose someone or something that you care about. Sometimes it is hard to think straight because you cannot take your mind off your loss. Usually, the load of sadness you carry after a loss will lighten over time, although for a really big loss, there may always be a little bit of sadness left.

Relationships bring happiness and fun much of the time. But tension or conflict in our relationships or relationships that break up can cause sadness too. People often feel sad when all is not right between them and their loved ones, when they are criticised or yelled at, when they feel a lack of support or badly let down.

Step Into Action

Remember, if you do not feel the lows, you will not feel the highs. Think of your emotions as a pendulum. The higher they sway in one direction, the higher they will sway back in another.

So when you are down, think about these things. No matter how hard you try to keep a smile on your face, you are always going to have ups and downs. If you do not embrace the hurt, it is impossible to learn anything new or to fully appreciate happiness when it does come along. Feeling sad is something everyone goes through, so instead of numbing yourself, take a moment to cherish the feeling. If not for sadness we would not have priceless works of art, beloved poetry or awesome music.

Action Plan

☕ Sit with the sadness, feel it, see where it is sitting in

the body and try to work through, utilising it where you can by understanding where it is coming from (as opposed to stuffing or medicating it!)

☕ When you feel sad, see if you can channel your feelings into something that will ultimately benefit you or make you feel better. Perhaps paint a picture, write in your journal, go to the gym, clear some clutter, clean the house, do something useful that will help to clear your mind.

☕ Perhaps take a long walk in the countryside or the beach. Reconnecting to nature often helps lift the spirits

☕ Meditate—go to a meditation class if necessary.

☕ Treat yourself to a massage or some reflexology.

☕ Find a good listener to talk it out of your body. It is important to choose someone who will simply listen without judging or trying to fix you and that it is someone who you trust

☕ Book a holistic therapy session that helps to move stagnant energy. A Crystal Therapy or Reiki session would help this. Always make sure your therapist is correctly trained and registered.

☕ Go with the flow, do not fight it or suppress it. Acknowledge it and then let it out.

Love yourself, you're worth it.

Managing Stressful Thinking

"The world we have created is a product of our thinking; it cannot be changed with without changing our thinking."
~Albert Einstein

S tress is a major component of every day modern living; the "wear and tear" our bodies experience as we adjust to our continually changing environment. It has physical and emotional effects and it can create positive or negative feelings. As a positive influence, stress can compel us to take action; it can result in a new awareness and an exciting new perspective. As a negative influence it can result in feelings of distrust, rejection, anger and depression, which in turn can lead to health problems.

Many of us believe that the stress we experience on a day-to-day basis is caused by outside forces. For example, our jobs demand a ridiculous amount of our time and the kids need our non-stop attention. It is easy to think that if we could just eliminate or handle the external factors, we would find the peace of mind we long for.

However, our stressful feelings are not always generated by external circumstances. Your busy life may seem like the problem, but really it is how you think that makes you feel overwhelmed.

When you worry about not having enough time to finish your work or do all the things you need to do, you start thinking: "I can't possibly get all these phone calls done by the end of the day. How will I ever write that report with all the meetings I have to attend? How can I get all my work done and also attend to the needs of the family, spend time with the kids, friends, etc? I'm going to have to work through dinner again."

These thoughts generate stress and as this happens, it often causes even more unproductive thinking: "I never have enough time to meet my deadlines." "I'm always behind schedule." "My office is a mess and I'm so disorganised." "The house is a mess." "The kids need so much time." "There is no time for me," etc. These negative thoughts affect your mood and as a result you feel annoyed, resentful and overwhelmed, as if the whole world is out to get you.

Stressful thoughts not only start to generate stress, but they lead to more unproductive thinking, which in turn leads you to worry that not only are you going to struggle with your current load, you are always going to struggle. Your mind moves from "I am behind schedule" to "I am always behind schedule" and "I will always be behind schedule."

Attempt to understand what is happening and perhaps you will notice a pattern. Your thoughts are directly linked to your feelings. If you think angry thoughts, you will feel angry. If you think about something painful, you will start to feel depressed. If you start to think happy you would actually begin to feel happy, but in your stressed state your mind will only fuel negative thoughts. Your emotional state always follows your thought patterns. Energy follows thought.

These low quality negative thoughts start to affect your mood, leading you to feel annoyed, resentful and overwhelmed. As a result, you waste time fretting, which only slows you down further. As the vicious circle picks up momentum it can seem like the whole world is out to get you. Stress, anger, tiredness and eventually illness set in.

Therefore, to eliminate stress, begin by eliminating your stressful thoughts. Let your feelings be your guide. The moment you notice uncomfortable feelings ask yourself, "What am I thinking about right now?" Then identify one or two thoughts. For example, if you are feeling rushed, you might be thinking about all the things you need to do within the next hour.

The next step is to change your thinking. Once you notice what thoughts are creating uncomfortable feelings, stop thinking those thoughts. Often merely noticing your thoughts will break the cycle. The moment you change your thoughts, you will enter into a calmer state and then you will be in a much better position to handle any situation. It takes a little practise but you can do it!

Often, when we are stressed, we wrongly believe that if we work faster or harder we will get everything done. However, this actually creates more stress and as a result you will feel even more rushed and anxious. It is a far better idea to bring yourself into the present moment, take a few deep breaths and then focus on just one thing, the thing you are currently doing. Do not think about all the other things that need to be done.

The most common and initial symptom of stress is muscle tension. For many this manifests across the shoulders, for others it is in the back or the legs. This is usually followed by one or more of the following:

 ☕ Irritability
 ☕ Inability to concentrate
 ☕ Feeling excessively tired
 ☕ Having trouble sleeping

Then, as the stress in our body builds, we begin to see more physical symptoms, such as headaches, upset stomach, rashes, ulcers, high blood pressure, heart disease and strokes.

So what can you do?

Try to understand what is happening to you and perhaps you will see a pattern. Your thoughts are directly linked to your feelings. If you think angry thoughts, you will feel angry. If you think about something painful, you will feel depressed. Your emotional state always follows your thought patterns. Energy follows thought. Therefore, if you want to eliminate stress, you must start eliminating your stressful thoughts.

Learning to manage stressful thinking takes time and practice but it works. When you change your thinking, you actually change your life!

Step Into Action

When you are feeling very stressed, take time out. This could be as simple as:

☕ Taking a 10 minute break from what you are doing.

☕ Find time each day to sit quietly just to be even if only for 10 or 15 minutes. Breathe in deeply, inhaling calm and with each exhale breathe out the stress you are feeling. You will feel almost instant relief doing this.

☕ Do your best to recognise your stress triggers and how your thoughts start to run when you are stressed.

☕ If you write them down you may see patterns, which

will help you understand what is happening to you and therefore how to change.

☕ Your thoughts are linked to your feelings, so remember if you think angry thoughts you will become angry.

☕ For every negative thought find two positive ones, even if not directly related, this doesn't matter as long as you change your train of thought.

☕ The next time your mind is tempted to run ahead, gently bring it back to the present by saying something to yourself like, "I'm doing this one thing right now and enjoying it." This way you will not only get everything done, but you will end up in a much better mood.

☕ Remove yourself from stressful situations wherever possible.

☕ Attend a stress management class to help you find ways to relax.

☕ Learn to meditate or attend a weekly meditation or relaxation class.

Love yourself, you're worth it.

Beating Fear

"Fear is the greatest destructive force to man's intelligence."
~Edgar Cayce

Fear is a huge issue in our lives. It takes hope away from us, it makes us doubt our purpose in life and it stops us from fulfilling our true potential. It can and often does paralyse us into a total lack of action.

The acronym that people love to use when defining fear is "False Evidence Appearing Real." All of us have experienced life-stopping terror and whether it is real or perceived, it can wreck lives. In order for us to live to our true potential all fear needs to be pinpointed, faced, challenged and then dealt with.

We all have fears, from creepy animals and insects to a fear of the dark, fear of failure, rejection, loneliness, poverty or death, a fear to learn and even the fear of success and a fear of the unknown. Those who fear failure stop themselves from doing what they really want to do. Yet they really fear success, for success may bring huge changes in their life. Although these changes may bring happiness and fulfilment, the fear of change holds them back.

Fear is an emotional response to the image of thoughts we are projecting in our heads. Whenever we picture ourselves being laughed at, rejected or failing miserably our nervous system responds and we start feeling anxious and fearful. Some people freeze in response to fear, others run away. Whatever the external reaction, the problem is that when we are fearful "we just don't think" and we react to circumstance instead of respond to it.

Go back to when you were a young child and you were holding that expensive ornament at grandma's house and she would say, "Now be careful and don't drop that." The moment you heard those words an image of yourself dropping it flashed through your mind and you started to feel the fear of breaking it. Then before you knew what was happening, you dropped it.

Every event in our lives happens first in our minds and then in reality. We actually manifest our worst fears, attracting them as we think of them. So now that we understand what fear is and how it materialises the things we fear the most, how do we get rid of it?

Most of our fears have a "worst case scenario" that really isn't so grim. An effective way to decrease fear and reduce our stress level is to imagine the worst thing that could possibly result from our fear. When we do this we face our fear in our mind and therefore render it powerless. Since this has been achieved in our mind and not in real life, it serves as a stress reliever and a training ground for facing it later in real life. When we start doing this we will see that what we feared is not as bad as we imagined. We tend to over-dramatise situations, but when we put them through a conscious analysis we are able to see them for what they really are.

Think back to when you were learning to ride your first two-wheeled bicycle. At first you were so scared of falling off that you rode too slowly so you could not find the right balance. Or perhaps you did balance for a few seconds but you over-reacted every time you swayed. Either way, you probably fell off many times. Each time you fell, the person teaching you to ride picked you up and dusted you down, gave you some encouragement and then you tried again. All the while, that person was right there behind you, holding the seat to help you balance. As long as they were there, you felt safe and your fears subsided.

You began to enjoy the feeling of riding the bicycle and positive emotions overtook the fear. It was ok, because someone was there to keep you steady and give you support. Or so you thought! Can you remember that moment of truth when you looked to your side and found you were alone? For a split second, the fear returned, but instantly you realised what you were doing. You were riding your bicycle unaided. You could do it. You had faced your fears and in doing so you realised there was nothing to fear after all, except fear itself.

When we face our fears we take away their power over us and we take control of the situation.

Every fear leads otherwise curious people to avoid exploration, learning and enjoyment in life. Maybe you have a gift or you are on the leading edge in your field of work, yet you resist marketing yourself as you fear success might change you. Perhaps you are unsure how you would maintain your integrity if you became well-known. But it could also bring other fears, like the possibility of discovering that people do not care about your work at all.

Rather than view the areas you fear as a total, why not break them down one at a time? Start with a few small activities then build your momentum and gradually overcome your fear.

Why do we fear?

If we were not afraid or fearful on occasion, we would not survive for long. We would walk into oncoming traffic, step off of rooftops, jump out of windows, tackle the person pointing a gun at our head and so on.

The purpose of fear is to promote survival. In the course of human evolution, the people who feared the right things survived to pass on their genes. In passing on their genes, the trait of fear and the responses to it were selected as beneficial to the race.

Step Into Action

When you fear something try these ideas:

☕ In your journal write down your fear or your fears.

☕ Say aloud exactly what you fear. "It scares me" or "What if I fail?" "I am scared of...."

☕ Daylight makes fear seem less frightening. Review your fears in the light of day then remind yourself that reacting is natural and you can deal with it.

☕ Talk to a close trusted friend or a therapist about what is stopping you from doing things or what you are scared about. Tell them you could use a helping hand to deal with it. Perhaps an extra telephone call to check in or help finding a therapist or the right help needed.

☕ Visualise a movie starring you as a capable and competent person who knows they can endure and win under upsetting circumstances. Pull your clip from past experience or script it from your imagination.

☕ Create a personal mantra, which you can use

everyday anywhere to ease your fears and reassure you. Say "I can handle it" or "I have no fears" to bypass the state triggering your fear.

☕ Physically moving helps you to stay strong and fit in order to deal with the situation. Perhaps walk around the block or in the park or do some relaxation breathing. It will calm your fears and take you forward.

☕ Acknowledge fear by naming it.

☕ Remember, everything is temporary and nothing lasts forever. This is just as true for good things as well as bad things. So whatever fear you are going through, remember it will pass.

Love yourself, you're worth it.

Do You Feel Guilty?

*"You wear guilt, like shackles on your feet, like a
halo in reverse."*
~*Depeche Mode, 'Halo'*

The dictionary defines the word "guilt" as a feeling of responsibility or remorse for some offense, crime, wrongdoing, etc, whether it is real or imagined.

Guilt is that nagging voice within us all that is like water upon a stone. It is meant to bring us to the realisation that there is a standard and we have fallen short, but whose standard is it? Who makes our standards? Who decides what is right and wrong? How many of us are put on guilt trips by parents or friends, spouses or siblings, or religious beliefs? Why do we allow it to happen? What does it do to us inside? Many often live a life consumed with it and sadly for no reason at all except an imagined incident.

We all feel guilt at times and it can be used as a reminder to improve things, but as in the words of Mark Balletini, "Guilt should be a momentary pang to spur one into corrective action. Anything longer is waste ...and worse, selfish." These words are very true and I carry them with me in my purse as a constant reminder!

Prolonged guilt, that is used to punish our self, is the most useless emotion we suffer from. It takes huge amounts of energy and it has often destroyed lives. The energy of it is toxic, just like the energy around unforgiveness, causing many problems, which will later manifest as illness.

Sometimes people carry guilt with them all their lives and as a result it destroys their life. When they tell the person involved what they feel guilty about he/she does not even remember the event! That is how toxic it is. There are, of course, other instances where great mishaps have happened, but a lifetime of feeling and suffering guilt does no one any good, especially the self. It also does not and cannot put a terrible incident right. It is a useless waste of energy that does nothing except make you feel awful.

I have had to work hard on guilt issues carried over from childhood. At times I still feel guilty for things I have nothing to do with. As a child, when things were going badly at home, I sometimes felt guilty for breathing and for showing any happiness. I am sure many of you feel the same. It affects us in lots of different ways.

Perhaps you messed up in love, at work, with money or with a friend. You ate chocolate when you were on a diet. You crashed the car and you could not even describe how lousy you felt. Maybe you lost your good credit rating, your closest confidante, even your health because one mistake created waves of consequences. So now what do you do? You understand we all make mistakes because this is how humans learn and grow and change, but you are finding it very hard to forgive yourself and to let go of the guilt.

Many of my clients are suffering from enormous guilt over transgressions large and small. "Forgiving" ourselves is one of the most challenging tasks in the human experience. Often we feel guilty because we 'think' we have wronged someone or something, when actually we have done nothing wrong at all.

If guilt means extending worry about what you have done, then it does not help. Buddhism stresses "not guilt but contrition" followed by developing an intention of restraint in the future. Simply put, you decide that you have done something wrong and then promise not to do it again. Sometimes, some tangible restitution is possible. For example, you can pay for damages or return stolen property. All that is left is an intelligent decision to face what has been done and make a commitment to break the cycle.

So how do you do it? How do you pardon yourself for your wrong doings compassionately? Before exploring your options for moving on, take a good look at why you did what you did. Are you just blaming yourself? If so, why? If you are being put on a guilt trip by someone, look at why you are letting them do this. Only you are responsible for you and only you can put a stop to it.

If you did do something wrong, perhaps you did not give enough thought about the consequences. Perhaps you had no idea that what you were doing could have any consequence at all. You did not leave the house that day thinking you would crash the car or mess your life up on purpose!

Most of us take a wrong turn because of a poor choice or we get caught up in situations beyond our control. We did not give something or someone in our life enough value or we gave them too much. Sometimes, when an opportunity arises to "mess up" we take chances because we hope no one will take notice. However, in reality it is pretty hard to fool people.

People in broken relationships often do drastic things for attention or love. They might attempt to bring their loved one back after a break up. They write emails and text messages they later regret and engage in obsessive phone calling, even after being asked to stop. In order to get past bad judgement and grow, realistic acceptance of the situation must occur first, followed by forgiveness of yourself and lastly asking for forgiveness.

When we really look at what we have done and if we meditate on it, past experiences will come up and it is a good idea to work with them. We may remember times when we treated others horribly by hurting their feelings, deceiving them, repaying their kindness with spite, manipulating them, cheating them. While regret for these actions is appropriate and often necessary, we often fall into guilt and shame instead. Guilt and shame are obstacles to overcome on the spiritual path because they keep us trapped in our self-centred melodrama of thinking "How bad I am" or "I have no worth." Regret, on the other hand, realises that we made a mistake and motivates us to refrain from acting that way in the future.

In moments of guilt, forgive yourself again. And, if it helps, remember that we all make mistakes, from world leaders to celebrities, as well as the people you may have wronged. It helps to remember that this is all part of the human condition. Living with guilt and shame is not living well, but forgiving ourselves and doing the best we can with it is what this lifetime is all about!

To help you put order back into your life, try the following:

Step Into Action

☕ Be honest, admit you made a poor choice and perhaps did not value whatever you lost. By doing this you will give yourself a chance to change and get it right in the future.

☕ Reflect on responsibility. Often it may prove that it was not your responsibility or fault! Blaming oneself for everything negative that happens is a form of ignorance and self-centeredness.

☕ Changing or accepting. If you can change the situation, change it! If you cannot change it for a good reason, accept it! Not acting where we can act may lead to frustration and guilt in the long run.

☕ Forgive yourself and then ask forgiveness of those you disappointed, even if they have no interest in giving you another chance. This takes courage; you may be rejected, dismissed, diminished or hopefully forgiven.

☕ Remember, making mistakes is an inherent human quality. If you do not make mistakes, you are definitely not a normal human being. If we are unable to forgive ourselves, we will never be able to properly forgive others.

☕ Make repairs where necessary, return money, stay late, work weekends to make up for a botched assignment, restart your diet, apologise, Whatever it is, do it!

☕ Learn from your mistakes. Spiritual growth cannot be learned without "messing up" along our path. Once you have done everything you can do, you will be on the right road. Talk to friends, family members or counsellors for reassurance and guidance.

☕ Do not allow others to put you on a guilt trip for any reason.

Love yourself, you're worth it.

Dealing with Betrayal

"Betrayal is about learning not to idealise external sources."
~Linda Talley

Betrayal is an odd thing. What is it really? The loss of faith? The loss of trust? The shattering of a sacred bond tying one person to another? A sacred contract broken?

We have all suffered the dreadful pain of betrayal or of being let down by those we love and trust. Some days the hurt is so intense that the truth can only be visited for short periods of time. If you are struggling with coming to terms with betrayal you will rotate through many feelings including shock, denial, anger/rage, extreme hurt/sadness, anxiety, emotional lethargy, social lethargy, changes in daily living activities, self doubt, insomnia, loss, disbelief; many of which are the symptoms of depression.

Betrayal is hurt that comes in many forms: a promise broken, a confidence violated, a boundary crossed, a lie exposed, dismissed commitments. Being hurt by another person is painful, but when we are hurt by someone we love and trust, the pain seems more intense because it takes us by surprise.

We are hurt when we least expect it by those we rely on. I am sure many of you have rolled up in blankets on the couch allowing no one, not even God, to comfort you. "Why didn't you warn me?" you ask in anger, unwilling to listen to the answer.

We often respond to these things in the same way as

the death of a loved one, shock and disbelief, tears, anger, despair. Questions fill our minds: "Why didn't I see this coming? What did I do to deserve this? How can I face the loss? Why didn't God protect me?"

Why don't we see it coming? The answer is simple—we are not looking. It is only dangerous people who arouse our suspicion. With such people we keep our vulnerabilities covered, ensuring we know the location of the nearest exit. But we do not do these things with those who we trust. That is the great thing about trusting someone, we do not have to be on our guard. So there we are, relaxed, at ease and unprotected when a horrible surprise occurs. A wife finds a receipt in her husband's coat pocket and realises he is having an affair; a business partner makes a decision with huge consequences for the company without discussing first; a young woman says yes to a date with a man she admires only to have the evening end in rape; a friend shares or violates a deep confidence, etc...

What did I do to deserve this?

When we are hurt, it is natural to look for someone to blame. Often our first response is to blame ourselves. We might says things like, "If I were stronger I wouldn't get hurt" or "see what a failure I am?" Sometimes we swing to the other extreme and blame the person who has hurt us. "She is insensitive. It's all her fault" or "He's cruel and self-centred. He is totally to blame for this mess."

Betrayal by another does not mean you have to betray yourself. It does not mean you are unworthy and unfit. It does not mean that you deserved the treatment you received. Blaming ourselves or others stops us from healing as it consumes our energy and overstates the negative. Blame makes reconciliation impossible. However, when we hold ourselves and others accountable for specific behaviour, we can be clear about the hurtful actions, recognise what can be learned from the situation and identify what steps can be taken to make amends. When we hold others responsible for what they have done, rather than blame them for all of our self-doubting feelings, we reinstate confidence in ourselves and we begin to heal our damaged self-esteem.

When you are betrayed by someone, it is highly likely that you will not easily trust them again. Trust is fragile and can be lost instantly. A long-earned trust may be eroded and then suddenly lost.

The rage and despair often associated with betrayal comes only when the experience is one of a profound violation of your faith in another person. The initial shock and anger can be quite draining, sometimes frightening.

In many cases, the draining feeling occurs when you cannot get an answer from them; why they did it, why they have not talked things through with you, etc. Or if you do get an answer, you know it is not the truth. Their words do not make sense and there does not seem to be a real reason or you feel that other people are forcing them into situations they do not really want to be in. Betrayal of a friend's feelings, intentional or not, can rip the friendship apart and leave both parties feeling empty.

How can I face the loss?

Betrayal signifies loss of trust, loss of safety, loss of predictability and maybe the loss of a relationship. The grief can seem overwhelming. Grieving the losses of betrayal are often compounded by the reactions of friends and families who are angry on your behalf. Well intentioned friends try to prevent you from feeling sad by pressing you to "not care" anymore. People will say things like, "Who needs someone like that in your life? Just forget about it and move on" or "Are you still sad about this situation? Why don't you go out and meet someone new?" While the intentions are kind, these statements only serve to further alienate the person who grieves. Whether the betrayal happened yesterday or way back in childhood, a sense of loss is involved and grieving is a necessary part of healing. Recovery from betrayal cannot be rushed by pretending it does not hurt or by diminishing the importance of the person you once trusted. Grief takes time and sets its own pace. It is important to take all the time you need to let the healing complete.

Previous experiences of betrayal, whether from infancy or adulthood can complicate the way in which you experience and heal and the length of time you take.

The next question we ask and often rant about is: Why didn't God warn me? Perhaps the most disconcerting consequence of betrayal is the spiritual wound that can result. The affects of betrayal are very similar to those of spiritual abuse. With betrayal, it is the quality of the perceived connection between the parties that determines whether the injustice feels like a betrayal or simply an unpleasant event or behaviour.

In the past, my relationship with God, the light beings of the Universe and angels has suffered serious blows from the experience of being badly let down. I felt angry that they had not warned me or given me additional insight so the ordeal could be avoided. I not only felt betrayed by a trusted friend, but also totally alone and worthless. I am sure many of you have felt this way too.

The only sure-fire way to avoid betrayal is to refuse to care about or trust anyone ever again. This path may seem wise when the pain is intense, but it is not a long-term solution and certainly not one I would ever recommend.

The most immediate effect of the betrayal of trust is the emotional impact on the person betrayed. Generally speaking, the greater the trust you had in the other person or institution the greater the impact their betrayal has on you, then the greater level of distress you will feel. A number of different emotions may be felt upon realising or feeling you have been betrayed. The most common is anger, although depending on the situation you might fear the loss of the relationship and wondering what you have done to deserve this treatment.

When someone betrays you, whether they really do whatever you are blaming them for or not, you lose trust in them; you lose a part of yourself, your security, your shield. It does not matter if the person really did what you are accusing them of or not. If you imagine someone betrayed you, it is every bit as bitter and emotionally true as if they had done what you imagined. You need to take the time to think seriously about what you now want from the relationship and the situation. You need to start to heal yourself and think about your feelings. You and the betrayer have both lost something and it takes time to fill that dreadful void and space. Learn from the lesson and move forward at your own pace and you will eventually come out stronger, no matter how painful it may have been.

If you betray someone, it is often best to come clean. Accept responsibility for your failure and personally apologise. Demonstrate how you will try to fix the situation, if you can, but do be honest as this helps both parties concerned.

Step Into Action – tips for starting the healing process

☕Acknowledge your pain, anguish and every other feeling you have.

☕Surround yourself with supportive friends/family.

☕Create a positive affirmation for yourself.

☕If you are choosing to end the relationship, writing a letter to allow your own release will be important for you (this is a letter that you will very likely not send).

☕If you choose to continue the relationship, make sure you set clear and specific limits for future interactions. Setting boundaries is essential.

☕Be sure to interact with at least one positive force in your life every day.

☕Allow yourself time to heal and learn. Forgiveness frees *you* from *your* pain.

☕Forgiveness will make you much stronger and release you from the toxic energy around the betrayal.

It is critical to remember during this healing time that:

☕Your trust has been abused and this is a very big deal. Recovery will take time.

☕You are *not* responsible for the betrayer's decisions.

☕You *can* heal. You are *not* alone. You are *not* "stupid." *you* did not create the betrayal.

☕You do *not* need to understand the betrayer's actions in order to heal. You *do* need to get lots more information if you are going to remain in the relationship.

☕You may never understand the betrayer's motivations.

You do not have to in order to heal. You *do* have to if you choose to resume/continue the connection.

☕ If you choose to continue the relationship, you *must* see *active* change in the betrayer towards a new, healthy, *honest* style of communication.

☕ You do have *choice power*. You *can* choose to allow healing. Healing takes time.

☕ History is *not* a guarantee of the future. The future *can* be different.

☕ You *can* and *will* learn to trust again, as soon as you relearn to trust you.

☕ If you have problems with forgiving or letting go of it see a therapist, or life coach.

☕ There are many meditation CD's available to help with situations such as these.

☕ Attend a workshop on learning to let go, forgiveness, or similar.

Love yourself, you're worth it!

Learning Forgiveness

*"Forgiveness does not change the past, but it does
enlarge the future."*

~Paul Boese

Forgiveness is powerful. To forgive and forget is to reflect love. Situations pass, they cease to exist, but they continue to live in the mind. Un-forgiveness and guilt are toxic, destroying our soul and those around us. To forgive is not saying what someone did to us was ok, but it releases the toxic energy in the situation and frees ourselves and others from the sorrow, bitterness and hate. Unforgiveness and its consequences takes almost 70 percent of our body's energy.

We all have people, institutions and situations that we need to forgive. All of us feel that at least one person has done us wrong, whether a sibling, friend, lover, teacher, parent boss or institution. The person may even be dead.

Often we stand in the shadow of bitterness, anger, hurt feelings, betrayal or resentment. We wait in misery and retell our story to friends and anyone who will listen, expecting them to sympathise with us.

Many years ago I met a really nasty 89-year-old. She was spiteful to everyone and hence very lonely. She lived in a home for the elderly and even there she managed to cause everybody problems. She told me she acted that way because when she was 10-years-old she was molested by an uncle. I jumped back at her by saying, "That happened to you seventy-nine years ago, when do you think you'll stop using

that as an excuse for your actions and behaviour today?!"
She just looked at me, shrugged her shoulders and hobbled
off. I remember thinking how sad it was that she has held on
to the pain and as a result her life has been a misery. What a
terrible waste of a life!

Until we learn to forgive, we carry the pain around
in our heart that a person or situation has caused us. The
more wrong we perceive that they did to us, the more
pain we carry. Years may have passed since the betrayal or
misunderstanding. Perhaps we have not spoken to a friend
for years and we cannot even remember why we do not speak
anymore. These little pieces of sadness or anger get under
our skin and into our bloodstream and run deeper through
the dark creases of our memory. Eventually they manifest
into an illness and can cause us all sorts of problems, such as
angry outbursts at inappropriate times.

Many people believe they can leave the past behind by
simply not thinking about it. However, the past, the present
and the future are all interconnected and one part cannot
exist without the others. When we push the past away
we stuff our feelings away, deep inside. We then become
disconnected and often fragmented. We no longer give our
feelings any validity and we stop trusting them. We insulate
and isolate feelings and emotions and therefore part of
ourselves, unable to deal with the emotional situations that
occur in our personal lives. We try to use logic to resolve
emotional situations and we usually fail miserably.

Logic and emotion must find a balance in our lives
if we are to be healthy. Denying how we feel about the
situations in our life is self-destructive. When we stuff our
emotions they do not go to a different place; they lie beneath
the surface, smouldering and waiting for an opportunity to

emerge. Unexpressed, repressed emotions eventually take their toll. Many people find themselves taking medication, such as antidepressants, just to get through daily life. Others go out and kill people, while some develop diseases such as cancer, arthritis, high blood pressure and diabetes to name but a few.

Forgiveness is the most powerful tool we have to deal with repressed emotions. We all feel victimised by the seeming injustices that take place in life, yet few of us do anything about those feelings.

Forgiving someone does not mean excusing them for what they have done to us. It means no matter how much we have suffered, we will release the toxicity of the situation. It means stopping the cycle of pain, sorrow, bitterness and guilt, moving on with our life and being happy, healthy and at peace.

By forgiving other people from the things that have occurred in life, our experience of life is transformed. But to forgive properly we must delve inside of ourselves and admit that we have been repressing our emotions. We must make a conscious effort to do whatever it takes to make peace with the past and ourselves.

If we hate someone and carry this feeling around with us for years we are not hurting the other person, we are only hurting our self. By holding onto this feeling of hatred we then attract others into our life with the same problem. Together we begin to feed off of each other's hate and then we start hating each other. This occurs because like attracts like.

Some people feel it is easier to forgive another for a wrongdoing while others easily forgive themselves. True healing can take place only when you forgive both yourself and the others involved.

Even if you do not feel like the other person deserves to be forgiven, remember there is another side to consider, the fact that *you* deserve to be forgiven. You owe it to yourself to be free from the hurt, anger and resentment.

If someone has truly wronged you, perhaps you will never be able to completely forget it. But for your own sake, decide which is more important, clinging onto the past or moving forward into a happy future.

Here is the good side to forgiveness: By relinquishing your need to hold onto bad feelings and negativity, your reward may include lower blood pressure, improved immune system response time, reduced anxiety and depression, increased energy levels and even weight loss as you let go of some of the emotional baggage that sits on the body in great lumps of fat.

By forgiving you free your mind, allowing an opening for better memories and moments to enter, hence resulting in a much happier, healthier, joyful and peaceful life. Forgiving transforms your life and the lives of those around you too.

If you want to truly forgive here are some useful tips:

Step Into Action

In your journal write down who you need to forgive. Do not forget to add yourself.

What do you get out of withholding the pain and unforgiveness?

What do you imagine life would be like if you let go and forgave?

How possible does that seem? Write down how it feels and what it does to your body and your emotions.

☕ What is the alternative if you do not forgive? What do you imagine your life to be like in five or even ten years time?

☕ If you have children, would you want to pass this feeling of negativity on to them? Is it worth them suffering as you have?

☕ If you decide to forgive (because it is your decision to forgive) try the next part of the wisdom growth plan:

☕ Tell your story one last time to a trusted friend or counsellor or write it down in full for yourself. The goal is to get it out of your system; it means a gentle recounting of what happened and how it affected you.

☕ Feel the pain. Really feel and experience your feelings so you can then pass through them. Avoid beating yourself up. Instead, simply feel with the intent of experiencing your way through and out of the pain. See where it sits in your body and write down the experience.

☕ Forgive yourself and others. Accept that you are not perfect, nor are they. As human beings we are prone to moments of greatness and not so great moments.

☕ Paint a different picture. Use the experience as an opportunity to see things in a new and positive light, as opposed to getting stuck in the tragedy. The moment is over. It is time for you to move on. You cannot change the past but you can build a happy future.

☕ Grow by appreciating the lessons learned from the situation and the potential for a new path. Life events change us on many levels. You can resist that fact or grow because of it. When you are ready, if you want, you can even share your newfound compassion with the person who once wronged you.

☕ Attend a workshop on forgiveness.

☕ Forgive yourself, you are worth it!

When I was finally ready to forgive, I asked the Universe to help and I came across the following ritual. If there is someone you would like to forgive, you might want to try it yourself.

☕ Set aside some time for yourself and perhaps light a candle.

☕ Think about someone you would like to forgive and repeat the following prayer out loud:

I fully and freely forgive X (mention the name of the offender). I let him or her go. I completely forgive the whole business in question. As far as I am concerned, it is finished forever. I cast the burden of resentment on the God within me. X is free now and I am too. I wish him or her well in every phase of life. That incidence is finished and God has set us both free.

☕ Offer thanks and get up and go about your business. When the event and/or person crosses your mind again (as it will), simply repeat: "I release this event" and then dismiss the thought from your mind. After a while you will find that the memory returns less often and soon you'll forget about it altogether.

Love yourself, you're worth it.

Overcoming Selfishness

*"Selfishness, if but reasonably tempered with wisdom,
is not such an evil trait."*

~Giovanni Ruffini

We all know selfish people who always put their needs first....it is self, self, self. Why can't we all be selfless and put others first? The world would be a much better place. Or would it?

How can you possibly develop spiritually, emotionally, mentally, physically or in any other way, if you do not focus on yourself? Much of what we are all trying to do is discover our true selves; to understand our own strengths and weaknesses; to work on our strengths and mitigate our weaknesses. Our personal development is central to everything we do.

Consider a person who gives up a flourishing career in order to devote their life to caring for a partner or family member with a long-term illness. We would probably say they were truly selfless. But what if they loved that person more than anything else in their life—more than life itself? What if they took that action so they could spend as much time as possible with the person who was ill, simply because doing that made them feel good? Is that selfish or selfless? Either way, is it a bad thing?

The dictionary definition of selfishness usually describes it along the lines of "an undue focus on one's own self interest, at the expense of others." In other words, a person who thinks only of themselves and I think we would all agree, that wouldn't be good. We need to take the time to consider the wants, needs and feelings of others too, but not all of the time. Spending our entire life putting others first will do nothing for our own self-esteem and so once again, the message is balance.

There are times when we should—we must—put ourselves first. We must feed and nurture ourselves in order to maintain our strength and grow. In doing so, we become better, stronger people who are more capable to assist and encourage others. We must look deep within ourselves and understand our own deep-rooted needs, our strengths and our weaknesses in order to understand who we really are and what our path is in life. We must have a rational self-interest in order to develop and maintain our self-esteem.

There are also other times when we must put the interests of others first, in order to maintain a degree of harmony and balance. We must use our inner strength to help encourage and nurture others. By allowing the needs and desires of others to occasionally take priority over our own needs and desires, we are not only helping to build the self-esteem of the other person, but we are also acknowledging that we are comfortable with ourselves and who we are. In doing so, we actually strengthen our own self-esteem or is that just being selfish?!

The really selfish people are the ones who cannot keep the selfish and selfless sides in balance. They are selfish even when they try to be selfless. An old friend of mine is the sort of person we would all love to meet on the road to Damascus. He simply cannot turn away from someone in need. He is always offering to give a helping hand to his colleagues at work if they have too much to do. Rather than pointing them in the right direction, he will take on their problems and sort them out. He really cannot do enough to help, even if it means he has to put in extra hours at evenings and weekends to get through all the work. A perfect example of a selfless person, right? Wrong!

He is known around the office as a soft touch. When his colleagues cannot be bothered to do something or when they are feeling a little pressured, they head straight for him with their sob stories. Of course, he buys them all and takes over. Meanwhile, his kids are growing up not knowing him. He has not sat down to an evening meal with his family for a very long time and to cap it all, his colleagues are seen as efficient effective workers and are promoted, while he is stuck in a rut. Is that the outcome he wants? Probably not, but by carrying out this role, he makes himself feel important. He believes his colleagues need him. He is a selfish person who is satisfying his own need to feel important while his family crumbles in front of his eyes. He needs to balance his own needs with the needs of his family and rationalise his self-interest.

So, how do we achieve this balance?

Step Into Action

☕ Take some time out to reflect on where you currently sit on the scale of selfish to selfless.

☕ Think about why you are where you are. What do you get out of being that way? Do you have a rational self-interest? Do you have no self-interest? Is your self-interest overdeveloped?

☕ Think about those who are close to you—family, friends and colleagues. How do you think they see you?

☕ Think about their needs and desires. Do you help feed them? A lot? A little? Not at all?

☕ Do you ever take real time out for yourself?

☕ How do you feel inside? Do you feel empty or do you feel fulfilled? Be truthful when you answer. Or is there a need inside that you are suppressing instead of feeding?

☕ As you build this picture, you will soon start to spot the gaps. You will begin to appreciate how you could change your behaviour a little in order to move one way or another back towards the middle of the selfish/ selfless continuum.

Love yourself, you're worth it.

Stop Playing
the Blame Game

*"When you blame others, you give up your power
to change."*

~Dr. Robert Anthony

We all play the Blame Game at times. We point our finger at other people for things that are going wrong in our lives because it seems easier that way.

However, have you ever noticed that when you point a finger at someone or something, three fingers point straight back at you? Try it and see. Point your pointer finger then twist your wrist ever so slightly, revealing three pinned-back fingers nestled in your palm. Those three fingers say, "The majority rules."

So now let us examine what it means to take responsibility for yourself and your life without blaming others.

Assuming responsibility for your life simply means that you take or possess the outcome of any situation. For example, if you are having a bad day and hit the car in front because "they were too slow," if you yell at your significant other because "they were insensitive," if your mother's cooking has made you fat, if you could not wear the dress you wanted because your mother or the maid did not iron it in time, then you are controlling your immediate environment. But instead of recognising this, we blame or point the finger at others, diluting our own power and ignoring the law of cause and effect.

We have all been given the ability to choose our path in life, but when it veers off in an uncomfortable direction, we are very quick to assign responsibility to someone else and we do this in all manner of ways. We blame colleagues when mistakes are made at work, we take our stress out on others, we find fault before we even look in the mirror. Rarely do we take a step back and think: could "I" have done something different? What will I do better next time? It is so much easier to blame others, yet everything starts and ends with ourselves and we are always part, if not all, of the problem.

When we take these hard glances at ourselves we become closer to evolving. Our growth experience has a direct relationship to how quickly we reach our destiny. You cannot grow if you do not own up to your actions and decisions.

He, she, it, they and external circumstances appear to teach us lessons. Our surroundings serve as a reflection of our selves. Picture a huge floor to ceiling mirror; that is what they are, they are *you*. Too much energy is wasted placing the blame on others, detracting from the value of the lessons or even the good you have done for yourself and others. The past is the past, the moment is now! Blaming or pointing the finger does no one any good. It does not put a situation right and only wastes a huge amount of energy, leading to unhappiness, bitterness and frustration!

Once you give your power to another, you miss the lesson and you continue to repeat it over and over again. Like any pattern, it will continue for as long as "you" allow it. Awareness does not emerge overnight, it takes time. But the sooner you realign your thinking to say, "I" take responsibility, own your life and admit "I" made a mistake,

I'll do better next time, the sooner you will feel better and then life will be a whole lot easier.

All you have is this moment and you need to live there now because everything is in the now. By replaying past events, grievances and injustices you bring on inaction, frustration and guilt. It is a broken mental record. So why not tear up your list (or lists) of who did what, when and why and bring on a whole new and happier life by stepping out of your comfort zone and quitting the blame game! Accept what has gone and embrace each new lesson or incident as an exciting opportunity to learn, grow and become a wiser, happier being. You will be amazed at how quickly life will turn around in your favour, bringing you more peace and happiness than you can imagine.

Step Into Action

☕ Write in your journal the times in the last week that you have blamed someone or a situation for something that has gone wrong in your life.

☕ Write down the times in your life that you have or still do blame others for what happened in painful situations that you may not have fully dealt with.

☕ Look closely at each of these entries and really think about the situation then take responsibility and learn the lesson.

☕ Whenever something upsets you or you start to point your finger at someone, remember that three of those fingers are pointing right back at you! Write down these instances, how you dealt with them and how it feels.

☕ If you know you should say "sorry" to someone, say

it and really mean it.

🍵 Do not beat yourself up about what you have written or the lessons you learn.

Love yourself, you're worth it.

The Art of
Non-Attachment

*"He who would be serene and pure needs but one
thing, detachment."*

~Meister Eckhart

We all become attached to things, whether material goods, people, ideals, etc. It is human nature to do so, yet our attachments often cause us stress, pain and suffering. Many spiritual books and teachers talk about incorporating the Buddhist belief and art of non-attachment into our daily lives as a way to relieve stress.

Practicing the art of non-attachment does not mean you stop wanting things; it simply means you are open to what the Universe has to offer you and the very real possibility that life can be much better than you have imagined.

Non-attachment teaches us how to get out of our own way and to stop limiting ourselves to our beliefs and outcomes of our dreams, goals and wishes. We often have very constrained ideas and belief systems that stop us from reaching our full potential.

The art of non-attachment does not mean you have to give away all of your possessions and move to a secluded mountaintop or into the middle of a vast wilderness.

Often, when we want something passionately we attach a whole set of specifics to our dreams, including exactly what we want and how we expect it to manifest. However when we do this the art of non-attachment suggests that we set ourselves up for suffering. A great example of this is love. Wanting love is a natural desire, but the struggle comes when we attach ourselves to the belief that a certain person offers the only path to achieving happiness in love or life. If you practice non-attachment you allow yourself to feel the desire, but you allow the Universe to bring it to you however it wants. The Universe will muster up far more than our limited minds can, bringing much more happiness into our lives.

This goes for everything in life. Our attachment to material possessions, people and outcomes often brings heartache and becomes heavy baggage. If we let go, detach and give up what is holding us back in life, allowing the Universe do its job, life becomes far easier.

Along with non-attachment comes the idea that you are exactly where you need to be right now. This is one of the best pieces of advice because really all we have is the now and everything is just as it should be.

So as of today relax into the flow of life, instead of struggling against the current. Eastern culture and belief tells us that suffering is a part of the human condition. Hence by giving up the struggle, we free up huge amounts of energy that can then be put to better use.

This does not mean that difficult situations will no longer arise because these are a part of life, but these situations will not be nearly as difficult if you do not fight against them. Simply accept that they exist and that you will counter them as they unfold. We all know our parents will probably die before we do, but it does not mean this looming suffering or sadness should interfere with enjoying every moment they are with us. By accepting the sadness that will come with their eventual deaths, we can let it go and enjoy the time with have with them.

Giving your full attention to what is right in front of you stops wild and random thoughts from interfering with your intentions. By living each moment as it comes (non-attachment), or living in the now, we engage that deep wisdom inside and we become more universally connected. If your next task is to wash the dishes then feel the bubbles, smell the soap and observe the details, instead of rushing through the chore to get to the next one. If you find your thoughts wandering to the future or the past, do not judge yourself, just notice the wandering and gently return to the matter at hand. In this way each moment becomes a form of meditation, connecting us with ourselves and the Universe. From this centred place we birth our own enlightenment, peace and contentment.

By choosing to accept rather than fight against your sadness and suffering, you will achieve a healthy type of detachment. By leaving the particulars up to the Universe you will realise the freedom of unlimited potential available by living in the moment.

Step Into Action

☕ In your journal write down anything you are holding on to for which you want the outcome to be a specific way.

☕ Write down any relationships you are holding on to because you believe they are the answer to your happiness even if they are causing you pain and suffering.

☕ Write down any situation you are holding on to, thinking it will bring you happiness or a better life.

☕ Explore why you feel this way and see where in the body you hold any of this stress or suffering. Write down whatever you feel and see where it takes you then make an effort to let go of the attachment.

☕ Then just see what happens and how you feel. The Universe will work with you.

☕ Do not be hard on yourself and do not suffer needlessly. Simply accept and let the Universe do the rest.

☕ Live in the present not in the future or in the past. Enjoy each day and what it brings.

Love yourself, you're worth it.

Vulnerability

"In the beginning, people think vulnerability will make you weak, but it does the opposite. It shows you're strong enough to care."

~Victoria Pratt

Being vulnerable is not being weak yet many of us think it is so we try not to show this side of us. If you look up the word "vulnerable" on dictionary.com it says: "Vulnerable means capable of or susceptible to being wounded or hurt." And that is very true. We are all capable of being wounded or hurt and most people on the planet have been hurt in some way.

Love is not just about giving. It is about loving ourselves and receiving love too. It is also about our vulnerability and not being afraid to ask when we need help. However, rather than asking for help, many people turn to alcohol, drugs, overeating or some form of self-abuse. This is because we do not want to show how vulnerable we are.

Yet for us to learn and grow spiritually and emotionally we must embrace our vulnerability, along with many other aspects of ourselves.

If you look at nature and the world around, you will notice that plants absorb nutrients from the earth, sun and sky. To get light they must sometimes withstand the heat, to get water they must sometimes weather the storm. To take what they need from the soil they must grow a root system designed to keep them stable in the shifting earth.

As humans, we are not much different. To get the physical, mental, emotional and spiritual nourishment we need sometimes we must also expose ourselves to certain dangers. Whether we like it or not, we are vulnerable and we need to accept that as part of the human condition.

If you take the idea of vulnerability beyond a definition of weakness or fragility and look at healthy vulnerability as a 'willingness' to take chances that allow for personal growth you will begin to understand how it can enrich your life. With the courage it takes to be as open and honest with yourself as vulnerability requires, you can see deeper inside yourself and then you will be able to expand your goals for the future and even open yourself up to love. You will also be able to start forgiving yourself for the things you think you have done wrong or all the things you feel you are incapable of. It will help you to stop worrying about what others think and you will realise your true value and worth. Everyone is vulnerable and once you reveal this life becomes far easier.

For some people being vulnerable is difficult because of their past experiences. A father may have left the family when the children were very young so the son might think he will never be a good father because he did not have one. A husband may have cheated on his wife so she feels she can never trust another man or vice versa. Our belief systems and values also get in the way of us showing our vulnerability. For others, even admitting to vulnerability is difficult. Some like to play tough, while others think they are like superman, impervious and impermeable; for them vulnerability is something to shut away and deny, but in actual fact it rules their lives.

To help yourself begin to be vulnerable start by recognising moments every day when it is safe to show or indulge in your own vulnerability. A healthy sense of openness to risk or vulnerability will help you to accomplish some if not all of the following:

☕ Help you to develop richer more meaningful relationships, including the relationship with yourself, which is the most important.

☕ Help to create less overall stress in your life as you will realise you do not have to be perfect all the time!

☕ Help to increase self-confidence, giving you wisdom and the freedom to make better or more beneficial choices.

☕ Allow more time to be spent pleasing yourself and less time pleasing others without feeling guilty.

☕ Free you from worrying about what everyone else thinks so you can start to be "you."

☕ Open you up to the possibility of greater emotional and spiritual growth.

☕ Allow you to reap the benefits that come with being able to share your feelings, helping not just yourself but others as well.

By accomplishing some, if not all of the above, you will become a better overall communicator, which will then enable you to share and empathise with others to a greater degree. Ultimately, this will give you a deeper insight into ways you can improve yourself and create the life you want.

Where does "vulnerable" fit in your life today? Are you facing your fears alone? Do you admit your vulnerability to friends, family or even to yourself? Are you truthful with yourself and with others? Speaking our honest convictions and feelings allows us to be vulnerable even if we think people may ridicule us.

Take the risk of being vulnerable. You will become a stronger person and as a result you will help not just yourself but others too. It is good to be vulnerable.

Step Into Action

⛾ In your journal write down your feelings about being vulnerable.

⛾ Explore the reasons why you feel that way and if you do not deal with it what will the final consequence be?

⛾ Each day recognise times when it is ok to show your vulnerability, taking small steps at a time.

⛾ Keep a note of how it felt to do this and the outcome. You will soon start to notice how much stronger you feel.

⛾ Treat yourself to a therapy session or a workshop on self-awareness and personal development.

Love yourself, you're worth it.

It Is Your Choice
to be Happy

*"No one is in control of your happiness but you; therefore,
you have the power to change anything about yourself or
your life that you want to change."*
~Barbara de Angelis

Each and every one of us has challenges to meet in our life and all of us have suffered hard times, sad times, times when we did not feel any happiness or allow it. We are human and it is natural to go through unhappy times, but how we choose to deal with our life and the challenges we face is entirely up to us. When trouble strikes or we fall upon difficult circumstances, we need to make decisions about how we will live with our new circumstances. We can look at the situation and choose to think that it leaves us unable to do anything except be unhappy and think "poor me," or we can look for the positive in the situation.

One thing is clear; we cannot control what happens in life. Life is ever-changing, obstacles appear at times and this is all part of our growth. If we resist and try to control everything life becomes harder and more difficult. Whatever life deals us we can manage our responses and our outlook on the situation. People often connect troubled or difficult times to a feeling of helplessness. It is true that the bigger the obstacle, the more important it is to detect the sliver of happiness lurking below the surface. Staying in a place of helplessness will hold you in that obstacle for much longer than necessary.

We all have the freedom of choice to select our thoughts. Therefore, you can decide to look at either the positive or negative side of a situation. But how do you choose? There is nothing wrong with wanting the best possible outcome, but when something less than that happens a quick decision needs to be made. Choose to be happy, look for the positive and do not let the negative get you down. An optimistic attitude increases your likelihood of success and promotes good health. Every time you choose optimism over pessimism your immune system is boosted. If you decide to choose unhappiness, negativity infiltrates your body and the odds increase that physical, mental and emotional illness will seep in.

It is always your choice how you feel and what you do; even a prisoner chooses his own thoughts. If you want to stay on the happy side of life, then simply choose to be happy. When something upsets you stop, take a deep breath or two and then pick "happy." It sounds simple but it works. By breathing deeply your body and mood stay positive and your head stays clear and is more prepared to tackle challenging situations. When you inhale deeply you breathe the life force energy that keeps you grounded and connected. Shallow breathing keeps you in your head and scattered.

Next, use your thoughts to feed the search for evidence of happiness. Dig deep into your memory bank and pull out at least two or three memories of things that make you feel happy. Hold these thoughts in your mind or write them on sticky notes and post them on the mirror, the fridge, the desk, in your i-phone, on your computer or anywhere else you will see them frequently. When your unhappy self threatens to overtake your happiness, swap the sad thoughts for happy ones. This will not be easy at first, but if you take steps daily it will soon become a way of life and happiness will dominate.

Actively avoid negativity and always look for the positive side of any situation. Wherever possible avoid negative people as their negativity is draining and destructive. When negativity creeps in, turn it around. Maybe you are planning to hold an outdoors party and on the day it starts pouring with rain. You hope to avoid cancelling since all the food is ready. Instead of choosing negative and thinking you will have to cancel, be creative and move the party inside! Clear out the living room, spread out towels and have a picnic inside instead. It could be even more fun and intimate this way. Turn the situation into a positive.

When something threatens to bring you down, challenge that thought by stating your new mantra, "I choose to be happy." It does not mean you are never going to be upset, it just means you are choosing not to get stuck in negative energy all day long. Challenge yourself to fight back every time negativity attacks.

See or invent a silver lining in everything then feed the silver lining with positive thoughts. Start to tell a new story about your life. Paint your life how you want it. Tell the story of how you want things to be and discontinue the story of how it was. Refuse the negative that has no part in your new happy story. Once you start doing this you will quickly feel the difference and your happiness will grow.

Start telling your new story and when you catch yourself slipping back into the old negative story, stop, breathe and shift back. It will feel strange at first but you will soon catch on.

Just remember, no matter what the circumstances, you have a choice about how you handle any situation. By making the decision to be happy you will see a healthier you and who wouldn't be happy about that?!

Step Into Action

☕ Choose to be happy and create the story to make it happen.

☕ Make your new mantra "I choose to be happy."

☕ When negative thoughts start to arise and overtake your new happy life, stop, breathe deeply then think of something that makes you smile.

☕ Leave sticky notes everywhere in your house with happy thoughts or things that make you smile or laugh.

☕ Avoid being around negative people and situations that bring you down.

☕ Do not listen to or read the daily barrage of TV news and newspapers, which only fuels the negative in the world.

☕ Choose to be happy and then you will be.

Love yourself, you're worth it.

Learn to Love "Yourself"

"The love you seek is seeking you at this moment."
~Deepak Chopra

If you want more love in your life, you are not alone. In many ways love is what life is all about. Empires have been built and destroyed for love. Thousands of books have been written on love. Thousands of songs have been sung. Beautiful poetry has been written and great works of art produced. Love makes the world and the Universe go round. We all want and need love in our lives and we all want to love and be loved.

Yet so often we forget the one person who can fill our whole life with love – 'you'! By opening your heart to life, to others and to yourself, you will grow love in every corner of your world.

Learning to love yourself sounds simple but it is one of the most difficult challenges of life. Learning to love yourself is about being totally at peace with your flaws and gifts, forgiving your mistakes and cherishing your triumphs. It is about taking care of yourself for the short and long-term, looking in the mirror and feeling content and comfortable with the person looking back at you.

When you love yourself, you will give yourself what you need. It may seem strange at first and feel slightly alien or uncomfortable, but you will soon get used to it. Then you will feel a whole heap better and you will want to continue to grow and develop, especially spiritually. You will become highly attractive to others because you will come to them out of wholeness, not neediness. You will be able to have fulfilling relationships and you will have no problem ending those which do not serve your highest growth. You will become a being of Light and love who has plenty of love to share with others.

To begin with, stop putting yourself down and start becoming aware of your strong points. Every aspect of your character can be expressed accurately in positive or negative terms. Start using more positive terms to describe yourself. When it comes to facts, accept them as such rather than trying to deny or change them. If you are a short person, you are a short person. Accept it. Do not spend your whole life trying to be a tall person. Instead, be the best damn short person the world has ever seen!

As you begin to accept yourself for who you are you will slowly fall in love with yourself. Once that happens, everything else will fall into place. When you start to love yourself, you will find yourself attracted to and attracting all different types of people. You are then on your way to attracting someone who will love you as much as you love yourself. We teach others how to treat us. If you love yourself you will not tolerate someone who does not love you back or who does not treat you as you deserve to be treated. Loving yourself first is the key to attracting loving and meaningful relationships.

If you are involved in an unhealthy relationship that brings negativity and unhappiness into your life, remove yourself from it. People come together in relationships for growth, not always for life. If a relationship sustains you, that is if you are both growing from it and if it has good loving energy, then it is possible that you are together for good. If not, either fix it or ditch it.

The only real responsibility you have is to work on yourself to raise your energy and that will become your gift to the world. Pull back from negative situations and negative people. You do not need to judge them or try to change them, just allow them to follow their path. You may want to give them a little shove, but if they refuse to move, you move instead. Look after and preserve your soul.

Consciously and subconsciously we are constantly trying to get people to love us. But in pushing for love and acceptance, we often compromise. We let others tell us what is wrong with us and we accept it, in the hope of winning their love. By doing this we are essentially saying (to ourselves and to the world) that we do not like ourselves very much. We hope for someone to make us okay so we let them tell us how we should be.

Take Action – Tips for How to Love Yourself

☕Ask for a list of things people like about you. Sometimes it can be hard to find things we like or love about ourselves, so ask other people who you trust to tell you the things they like about you. This is not a replacement for your own love; it is a first step in learning to love yourself. You may need to hear the things other people like about you before you can value them in yourself. If hearing what people like about you is hard, ask them to write it down for you or leave it on your voicemail so you can read/listen to it repeatedly. Listen or read as many times as you can. Even if you do not believe that someone can like a certain thing about you, or you do not believe it exists, trust that your friend sees and values it.

☕ Make a list of all the things you like about yourself and be as honest as you can. Modesty will not help you here, neither will old critical messages. If you are having trouble finding things you value about yourself, think about the things you value and love in your friends then see if those things exist inside you too. Often, they do.

☕ Get out your journal. Write down the things your friends say in it so you have a record of them. If you start to hear critical voices inside your head, go back to those entries and remember that you are loved. You can look at this any time you are feeling down or critical about yourself or any time someone says something that triggers self-criticalness. Look at this good-things-about-yourself list as frequently as you can. It may seem silly, but repetition does make a difference. Think of the impact one critical phrase said by a parent over and over to a child can have. Try to give that child inside you at least one truly loving phrase that s/he can hold on to.

☕ Make it a part of your daily routine to praise something about yourself or something you like about yourself. In this society we are taught that praising ourselves is selfish and wrong, but actually it is a healing action that nourishes our self-worth making us truer to our selves, which then spreads to others. Try to think of something you like about yourself or something you did today that made you or someone else feel good. Give yourself the kind of warm praise that you would offer to a friend.

☕ Love yourself like a friend. Close your eyes and think of a person you deeply love and trust. Think about all the things you love and appreciate about them. Notice how that love feels inside you and how good it makes you feel. Now turn it around and be your friend, feeling that same deep love for you. Trust it and feel it. Let yourself see "you" through gentle eyes with compassion and love, even if you can only do it for a moment. Let yourself receive the love and feel the warmth move through you.

☕ Make a note every time someone says something nice about you. Every time someone tells you something about yourself that makes you feel good, write it in your journal.

☕ Have compassion for yourself. If you are feeling really judgemental about something you have done or said, try to understand where the judgement is coming from. Not the immediate, surface answer, but an answer from deep inside. Are you afraid of something or are you feeling insecure? Do you think you did something "wrong" or are you hearing the judgement of a voice from your past? Try to connect to that feeling and really listen to where it is coming from. You can also think of a friend having acted as you did. Imagine how you would feel towards them and how you would readily forgive them if there was anything to forgive. You probably would not even find it bothersome. Try to feel that same love and compassion for yourself.

☕ Use affirmations. You probably do not like saying affirmations, but if you hear good things about yourself repeatedly, some of them will sink in. Write out strong, loving words to say to yourself, even if you do not fully believe them. Some examples are:

☕ "I utterly and completely deserve love and kindness."

☕ "I am a very loveable person."

Put those affirmations in places where you will see them every day and do not forget to read them! Read your affirmations slowly and really let yourself feel them.

☕ Recognise self-critical messages. It is easy to let old critical voices and messages play in our minds. Often we may barely recognise that they are there or we do not really listen to them, but they continue to impact how we feel and think about ourselves. Notice the next time you hear a small (or very loud) voice inside your head criticising you. Be aware of what it is saying to you and try to talk to it. Ask it why it feels it needs to say those things. Is part of you trying to protect you? Or perhaps that part of you felt it had to take on the messages you heard as a kid. Remind yourself you no longer need to do that to survive. You are free to make up your own mind about yourself.

☕ Allow yourself to do comforting and nurturing things for yourself. Let yourself feel how good you feel when you do those things and tell yourself that you deserve to feel that way. Gradually you will find that the more nurturing and comforting times you have, the more you will seek them and they will build a good feeling inside you.

☕ Ask yourself what you need to do. Some of these things will work really well, while others may not quite fit for you. Take a moment to be quiet and ask yourself, "What can I do to help myself feel more compassion and love toward myself?" Don't force an answer, just let it come from inside. If you find it hard to hear the answer that way, try writing down your question and then your answer. See what you come up with.

Love yourself, you're worth it.

Affirmations to Love Yourself

"I have arrived. I am home. In the here. In the now, I am solid, I am free. In the ultimate I dwell."
~Thich Nhat Hahn

We all have the desire to love and to be loved. This passage from *A Return to Love* by Marianne Williamson describes our need for affirmations and to recognise ourselves as whole: *"Our deepest fear is not that we are inadequate. Our deepest fear is that we are powerful beyond measure. It is our light, not our darkness that most frightens us. We ask ourselves, 'Who am I to be brilliant, gorgeous, talented, fabulous?' Actually, who are you not to be?"*

Statements that inspire you to reach for your greatest potential often work better than affirmations. For an affirmation to manifest in your life, it must resonate with you so strongly that the vibration from it is carried forward into the way you behave in the world. Such affirmations have very beneficial effects because they are important reminders when wrong thinking clouds your vision and doubts set in.

They can help ground you and bring you back to your centre. They also give you the courage needed to go forward into difficult or frightening territory.

Affirmations can be found just about anywhere...in books, movies, speeches, poems, conversations or websites. The first step is to write down affirmations that resonate with you. Keeping a record gives them a place in your life.

Say the affirmations to yourself silently or aloud and do not worry what other people think. Many people find that reciting an affirmation while looking in a mirror helps to reinforce its power.

Tell yourself daily that you are worth loving, that you are beautiful and perfect just the way you are. Say these statements looking in the mirror until you really believe them.

Become aware of what you tell yourself daily and as soon as you realise that you are being hard on yourself stop and start afresh.

Here are some affirmations that might help:

"Om Namah Shivaya" (I honor the God within me).
~*Siddha Yoga*

"No one can make you feel inferior without your consent."
~*Eleanor Roosevelt*

"What you think of me is none of my business."
~*Wayne Dyer*

"What I am looking for is already in me."
~*Julie Lomas*

Action Challenge

☕ Re-read the above section and mark the area which is really appropriate for you then write it down.

☕ Find and write affirmations that work for you! They have to resonate with your very core.

☕ Become more aware of what you are saying to yourself. Every time you say something negative, write it down so you will start to see a pattern of why you do it.

☕ As soon as you say something negative or beat yourself up, stop then say something loving about yourself.

☕ Look in the mirror everyday and have a truly loving conversation with yourself.

☕ Know that you are perfect and unique; no two people can ever be the same.

☕ Everyday do something just for "you" even if it means sitting in the car to listen to your favourite song on the radio.

Love yourself, you're worth it.

Making Friends
with Change

*"If you don't like something change it; if you can't change it,
change the way you think about it."*
~Mary Engelbreit

One thing that is certain in life is the inevitability of
change. Repression and resistance to change is futile
because sooner or later it will happen.

Change is like a river, constantly flowing and moving
things around. The river of life is constantly bringing you
ideas, people and situations and each one is an opportunity
to grow and learn. Our lives are continuously changing
from birth to death as we move through childhood, puberty,
adulthood and old age.

Most of us cope with these changing cycles without
much difficulty because we understand them. We know
these cycles cannot be stopped as they are the essence
of life itself. However, we often have much more difficulty
accepting unexpected or unwanted change. This usually
takes us outside of our comfort zones into the realms of the
unknown. We then tend to resist change as we try to cling
onto what is familiar, often creating much unnecessary pain
in the process.

I am sure many of you resist change at times and have
felt pressured to change old ways of being which are no
longer appropriate as you grow spiritually. As the world

changes we must change too and right now the world is changing at a rapid rate.

The huge transformational shift taking place on earth right now is raising our consciousness, shaking our values, old belief systems and patterns. The old ways are falling away and new ways are emerging. These are much needed changes that many will resist and struggle with, as their whole lives and lifestyles change. But it will happen regardless of struggle or resistance. Therefore, it seems there is no better time than now to make friends with change. Change is a constant that we cannot stop. Change is happening now.

Remember that change is really only a challenge to what we are used to and to our personality, which likes to think it has control over the direction of our lives. However, it is the real you—the soul—not the personality that is the guiding force in your life.

When you next face what looks like a particularly challenging requirement to change, sit and think about it or meditate on the situation until you see the higher purpose of this challenge from the perspective of your soul.

This will not necessarily silence your personality's resistance, but it will begin to bring your personality into alignment with your soul, giving you a firm foundation to work from. It will also help you with the resistance, fears and worries it brings. You will start to see things differently and accept that you need to flow with the change. Change will always happen. How you deal with it is your choice. So why make it difficult?

Resistance to change is nearly always based on the events of the past, either consciously or subconsciously. Take some time out and quietly view the issues that the situation brings up. Ask yourself what old thought patterns and emotions are being activated? How valid are these in the current situation?

Next, commit to the present, to the now! Bring yourself into a state of acceptance that whatever is happening is exactly what should be happening.

As hard as it can be, do not argue with reality as that only makes things more difficult. Most of us find it very difficult to stay in the present moment when we feel challenged. It is a natural reaction, but we must do so in order to deal with difficult change. It is ok to drift off for a short while to recuperate and give our self breathing space, but only for a short period.

Let the future unfold with ease and grace. Life is in a constant state of change and we must accept that we have little or no control over 99.9 percent of it. By letting it flow we will live a happier and more abundant life.

Step Into Action

☕ In your journal write down your reasons for the resistance to the change.

☕ Look at the patterns or emotions from the past that are being activated.

☕ Write how they are valid to the current situation. Doing this will help you to identify the issue and let it go.

☕ If you have a problem letting go of the old issues, look at the reasons, meditate on each one and see clarity in the reasons.

☕ Commit to living in the present. Do not argue with reality.

☕ Let the future unfold with grace and accept that

resistance is futile.

☕ Nurture and love yourself.

☕ If you are really struggling with the change, book a coaching or therapy session.

Love yourself, you're worth it.

The Art of Compassion

"Compassion is incomplete if it does not include yourself."
~Buddha

Compassion is an emotion that is a sense of shared suffering, most often combined with a desire to alleviate the suffering of another. Compassion usually arises though empathy and it is often characterised by the actions of a person seeking to aid the one they feel compassion for. Compassion connects us to others as we aim to understand their point of view, notice their suffering and become sensitive to what they need in moments of difficulty or despair.

It is the ability to walk in another person's shoes. It is not sympathy, but the capacity to see others and their circumstances for what they are. It is the understanding that if we look at another with a spiritual heart, we can help them to embrace the best path without interference, lecture or judgement. We must have the strength to allow them to go through whatever is best for them, but to be there as support and comfort.

The Dalai Lama once said: "If you want others to be happy, practice compassion. If you want to be happy practice compassion."

Compassion is not attempting to fix someone or making their well-being a personal project by smothering them with sympathy or kindness. To be compassionate we may feel the need to alleviate another's suffering, but we cannot do it for them. Instead, the best we can do is simply to listen or be there for them.

Unconditional love and compassion go hand in hand. One of the main goals of being human is to develop compassion and unconditional love. To live a truly compassionate life we must give ourselves the same gift of loving kindness.

For the majority of people, compassion comes with age and experience. Some people never learn the lessons of compassion. The key to learning compassion is to be compassionate with yourself. In general we are way too hard on ourselves, usually because we think too much. We need to stop being in our heads and instead come into our hearts! When we do this and understand this we are able to help other people come into their hearts too. Then our answers are far kinder and more compassionate than before.

The key to developing compassion in your life is to make it a daily practice.

Step Into Action – to help you learn the art of compassion

These suggestions for compassionate practices can be done anywhere, anytime, at work, at home, while travelling, in a store, at the home of a friend or relative. With practice you can not only be compassionate throughout the day, but also throughout your lifetime.

☕ One of the first steps in cultivating compassion is to develop empathy for others. Many of us believe that we have empathy and on some level we nearly all do, but often we forget it as we are so busy with our own lives.
☕ Put yourself in the shoes of someone who is suffering. If something terrible has happened to them, try to

imagine the pain they are going through and in what way they may like help or understanding.

☕ Reflect how you would feel if someone desired your suffering to end and acted on it.

☕ Instead of seeing differences between yourself and others, try to recognise what you have in common. We are all human beings. We all need food, shelter and love. We all want attention, affection, happiness and many other things. Reflect on these commonalities and ignore the differences.

☕ When you meet new people mentally remind yourself things such as, "This person is seeking happiness in their life just like me, they don't want suffering in their life any more than I do. Just like me this person has known sadness, loneliness and despair."

☕ Once you can empathise with another person and understand his humanity and suffering, the next step is to want that person to be free from suffering. This is the real heart of compassion, the definition of it.

☕ Open your heart to that person and if you feel you want their suffering to end, reflect on that feeling. That is the feeling you want to develop. With practice, that feeling can be grown and nurtured.

☕ Once you get good at this, practice doing something small each day to help end the suffering of others, even if it is in a tiny way, such as a smile, a kind word, running an errand or talking about a problem. Practice doing something kind to help ease the suffering of others.

Love yourself, you're worth it.

Learning to be Patient

"Our patience will achieve more than our force."
~Edmund Burke

H ave you ever pulled an Angel or Oracle card that says "Patience," rolled your eyes and said, "How long do I need to be patient for? I've been waiting for so long." I know I have done so regularly and I still dislike getting that card even though it is usually totally correct.

A survey by a national newspaper set out to discover why levels of anger were rising in the world. The results found that the main underlying cause was not having one's expectations and desires fulfilled fast enough! In other words, impatience with events, governments, other people, delivery services, bus services, train services, airlines, etc. This may not come as a surprise considering the hurriedness of modern day life. The email addict is always looking for the next opportunity to access their inbox, the boss always wants everything done yesterday, the shareholders want their profits instantly and so on.

While most people admit to being impatient in some area of their life, not many know how to free themselves from their quickening anxieties. The majority would rather not be so impatient, but the only problem is they want whatever it is now. Obviously restoring a little more patience to your life will require some patience!

It is said that patience is a virtue and a power too. Patience tells us that the journey of a thousand miles begins with a single step and that we get there one step at a time. Patience teaches us not to rush, knowing that there is a reason and a season for everything. It enables us to smile at the challenges, realising there is an answer to every problem. And even though we cannot see it yet, there is awareness that within every crisis lays an opportunity.

It is said that patience is a reflection of the peaceful mind. A peaceful mind is able to cope with all situations without growing disturbed and agitated. It calmly accepts the resolution of circumstances and acquires the power to deal with all situations.

Patience is one of those virtues which can transform a moment of high anxiety into quiet relaxation, a rush of mental agitation into the smooth flowing river that life can be. In the presence of a patient person we are surrounded by an aura of calm as we are pulled into the tranquil light of their unhurriedness. Even when they are busy, the quality of their busy-ness still radiates patience. Perhaps the secret is to, "Adopt the pace of nature: her secret is patience." Nature is almost always patiently busy, either visibly or invisibly.

Have you ever played a waiting game? I am sure you all have. We learn to play it from childhood. It is easier for some than others. People often do it in their relationships. Work teams do it when waiting for the right time. Have you ever consciously decided not to hurry something, somehow knowing deep within that everything will happen in the right way at the right time? The older, wiser and mellower amongst us tend to do this. Have you ever decided not to rush somewhere realising you cannot make yourself arrive faster than your mode of transport and you cannot control what gets in the way? Bus and taxi drivers learn to do it, even racing drivers have to do it.

So how can you be more patient? Can you just become a patient person? Can patience be a permanent thread woven through your personality? How do you create patience?

You could start with visualisation. Being patient is a creative process. The first step is to admit and acknowledge that your impatience is entirely your own creation. It is not the late train or failing delivery service; it is you that makes you impatient. You have created and sustained the trait so you can create and sustain patience. Like all your other creations, the process begins on the screen of your mind. That is where you conceive, believe and achieve patience in rehearsal before you step onto the stage. That is where you create both the image and feeling of being patient. To do that, you will need to draw on a variety of inner resources and feelings, which are available to us all. One of them is Peace.

Take a few deep breaths then go within and feel your inner peace. This is the peace of your heart in your heart, the peace that can never be taken from you. It is part of you but you can lose awareness of it and most of us do. Peace is the foundation energy of patience. If you cannot draw on your inner peace, patience will be almost impossible to achieve.

The next thing is "acceptance." Your inner peace can only travel from your heart to your mind when you no longer want to change what is. The moment you accept everyone and everything as you find them, without resistance or judgement, the moment you are able to embrace life in its totality. That alone is quite a challenge as we have a tendency to spend too much time and energy in our minds. From there we judge others and "fix" the problems of the world, under the illusion that it is our job and that we can! With this peace and acceptance will then come "contentment." Your peace and acceptance are like two primary colours, which when mixed together create contentment. You cannot be patient unless you are content in yourself, with yourself and with the world in this moment now. This also requires the realisation that there is only ever now. Only then will all attempts to escape into the future or hide in the past end. At times this is very hard to do and most of us struggle with it. Contentment is neither passive nor submissive, but very available to us and from it comes wisdom. You will then hear and feel the wisdom that comes from the truth you already hold deep in your heart. Your faith in life will emerge and you will know that everything is unfolding just as it should be, creating spiritual freedom.

Impatience is the absence of faith, the confidence that life will show up with exactly what you need when you need it. Once you fully realise this you then know that all you ever needed is already within you. Life will cease to revolve around waiting impatiently for what you want or expect. Faith does not depend on a clever head, only belief in the self and the strength that lies within.

Impatience makes us "a patient" in life. Each moment you attempt to force an outcome, each moment of anxious waiting or expectant desire, is simply making a wound in your life and giving yourself more stress, which will eventually require the healing that comes from peace and acceptance.

Perhaps the most valuable lesson of the virtue of patience is its ability to bring wisdom back to life. In most western cultures, when things appear to be going wrong, we have the tendency to shout, "Don't just sit there, do something!" Whereas, in the ancient east the tendency was to whisper, "Don't just do something, sit there." In such moments we are acknowledging the need to allow a deeper wisdom to inform our responses. Wisdom, however, does not appear in our consciousness on demand. An invitation must be sent to our heart and then a patient wait is required before a reply is received. Perhaps this is why the wise and the patient know that patience and wisdom are both the best of friends and inseparable companions.

Step Into Action

☕ Are you a patient or impatient person?

☕ Think about what areas of your life are you are currently impatient with and why? Write them down in your journal.

☕ Does your impatience ever get you into troublesome situations?

☕ Which of the above ingredients of patience do you think are missing?

☕ When you have decided which is missing, on separate days during the coming week or month contemplate it, reflect on it, explore its meaning and see what it awakens, shifts and even heals within you.

☕ By writing them down along with any other issue that comes up, you will begin to see how patient you can become in that time.

☕ Take some time out and meditate. This in itself can bring you an inner calm and peace.

☕ Don't berate yourself when you slip up and act impatiently, see what it was that triggered the impatience and how it made you feel or if it caused the situation to be worse. Learn from the experience and then let it go, next time you won't be so impatient.

☕ Remember impatience doesn't get anything done any quicker, it just causes you or those around you more stress and disturbs the balance of life.

Love yourself, you're worth it.

What is Passion?

"Life is a paradise for those who love many things with a passion."

~Leo Buscaglia

Passion is a gift of the spirit combined with the totality of all the experiences we have lived through. It gives us the power to live and communicate something we feel is great. It is most evident when the mind, body and spirit work together to create, develop and manifest our feelings, ideas and most sacred values. It enables us to overcome obstacles (both real and imagined) and to see the world as a place full of wonderful potential. Someone with passion about something is able to look at every occurrence and see what can be, what should be, or what will be.

Your passions can drive you to action and get you out of bed in the morning. Passion is a driving energy force and can sustain during periods of adversity, disappointments and even disaster. Your passion stirs something deep inside you. It motivates you and lets you work and live to your highest potential.

You can be passionately against something, as well as passionately for something! It is good to know when you are passionate about something, what lies at the heart of that passion.

Passion has its own energy, which is very real, very observable, very transferable and at times addictive. The best thing about passion is that you cannot fake it!

Passion is a powerful tool in determining the authenticity of an individual. Passion supersedes the wants of expensive designer clothing and luxury goods and vehicles. It strips away the thin veil that separates what is said and what really is.

Passion is energetic, dynamic and contagious. It can be the force for movement and success. When people are passionate about something it is almost infectious when they speak of it. Yet many people run away from personal and professional passion because they are afraid of being burned or hurt or laughed at. Past relationships that ended in pain, trusts and confidences that were betrayed, risks they took. Most people have touched the fringes of true passion, even if only for the briefest of moments, often at unexpected times in their lives. However, many stay away from being passionate about something they believe in, opting instead for a more predictable existence. They do not want to take a leap of faith and immerse themselves in their deepest joys and motivations, so they insist on hiding inside a safety bubble, a lifeless and colourless world where nothing new ever happens and the only thing they can rely on is that tomorrow will be the same as yesterday and that today will be more of the same.

Then there are those with passion in their lives, who fight their causes and follow what makes them happy. Many believe that if you have no passion you have no life and you might as well be dead. If we think of the great musicians and artists that we all know and love, all of them had real passion. They believed in music and art and they lived their lives for it. I know a great photographer and he is always telling me you can have passion without art, but you cannot have art without passion. He loves and lives his work and it is very beautiful.

Think of all the great world leaders and figures in history, good or bad...they all had passion. They believed and lived what they believed with passion; it drove them. They led armies and conquered countries, they led armies and liberated countries, they created revolutions of many types. They were able to do this as they had passions and drive and really believed the people they followed.

I believe we all need a global return to passion, to basic spirituality, belief in ourselves and the right to owning and living those beliefs.

How wonderful it would be if we were all be receptive to experiencing every second of every hour of every day to its fullest, enjoying our lives, knowing who we are and realising that we all have worth, meaning and the right to be in our own "I am" presence.

Beyond the physical and the emotional there is also the spiritual. Perhaps we may find the real meaning of passion in the territory of spirit. The root meaning of enthusiasm lies in the Greek term entheos, which describes the natural, unhindered energy of spirit. It means to be filled with the "divine energy." When our core energy, our spiritual energy, moves out into the world in a natural, creative way, we experience and feel what is known as enthusiasm. We all know this experience. Think of a time when you were being creative. Notice your enthusiasm during the process. Notice your enthusiasm as you spoke about your creative experience to others. And notice your enthusiasm to return to create some more. Notice, as you speak about that creative experience with enthusiasm, how the people you were talking to really listened. All artists know this kind of enthusiasm and it means they have found their passion.

We are all artists, as we all get to create our own lives. We do this by creating thoughts, decisions and building relationships with others. So why do so many of us lack enthusiasm in life; why do we lack 'a passion' for living? Why do we create desires, anger and sorrow instead because these kill our enthusiasm. They destroy our passion for living. Finding your passion in life and living enthusiastically, requires a degree of self-awareness and self-understanding. It means realising that life is a creative process and the energy required to fulfil that process is unlimited in supply within your own heart. When it is discovered you will know enthusiasm, you will be enthusiastic.

It should be a crime to bottle up the passion you felt as a young person so that you will fit into a controlled corporate environment or circle of associates. Passion shapes our existence, fuels the fires of inspiration and opens the heart and mind to changes. It is food for the soul, a spark that illuminates our purpose and mission for being here. Passion is yours to experience and revel in. Passion is your birthright. It is within you. It is yours to discover and master.

Step Into Action

In your journal, make a list of the things in life that you really believe in that you are passionate about.

What do you really enjoy doing?

What makes you the happiest? What makes you the angriest? Write next to them why?

What do you care deeply enough about to desire to influence other people?

What kills your passions? What holds you back? Is it fear or values or self-limiting beliefs.

☕ Pick one of those things and start to live that passion.

☕ Stop bottling up your passion or belief; start to live the truth of who you really are.

☕ Start to believe in yourself and your passion and stop conforming to the corporate world or those around you and what you think people want from you instead of being you.

☕ Find others who are passionate about what they do and watch how they fulfil their passions and truly live. Learn from them.

☕ Live your life with passion and enjoy it to the full.

☕ If you have difficulty expressing what you are passionate about book a coaching session with me or a professional life and business coach.

Love yourself, you're worth it.

Knowing What You Want

"This time, like all times, is a very good one, if we but know what to do with it."

~Ralph Waldo Emerson

How often do you feel like you want to make changes in your life, but you are not sure what those changes are or how to go about it?

If a friend asked you what you want from life right now how would that make you feel? Would you even be able to answer? Ask yourself that question right now. See how it feels and what answers come to you.

It is possible that this question will make you feel uncomfortable for a moment or two. If it does, ask yourself why. Is it because you do not really know what you want? Are you too afraid to express your wildest dreams in case they are never fulfilled? Or maybe you think they are unrealistic?

The reason why that question is so challenging is because it is not a stand-alone enquiry. It brings many emotions to the surface. The majority of people have forgotten about their dreams and desires either because they live in a stressful environment or because they have simply forgotten who they are and what they would like.

If you cannot answer the question straight away then look at ways to do so. Sit and contemplate, look back through old journals and see what you have always dreamed about. Ask friends, family, relatives and colleagues what you used to say you wanted from life or dreamed of doing, having, being.

Once you have discovered what you really want, take the right action to get it by following these steps:

In your journal make a list of three to five of your most wanted desires. For example, to lose 20 lbs in weight, go on an exotic holiday, buy a new home, move jobs, start a new relationship, start a new business, take up a certain hobby, write a book, achieve financial independence, sail around the world, climb a mountain, learn a new skill, etc.

Then ask yourself, "If I do this or achieve this, what would it give me?" Think about the desires on your list and figure out what you would stand to gain from each. Perhaps it would improve your health, help you find a new job, bring you peace of mind, help you find inner peace, improve your confidence, give you a sense of fulfillment, etc.

Now ask yourself, "What do I need to do to make at least one of these desires happen within the next 12 months?" Write down everything that comes to mind. If your desires are big things, such as learning a new skill, changing your line of work, improving your health, or climbing a mountain then break down your actions into stages. Perhaps you could begin by finding out about a course, joining a slimming club, cutting out sugar or getting fit. Try to focus on only one step at a time.

Allocate some time each day for yourself or your

new project.

Now you know what you want and why you want it, set up some strategies to help you achieve it. Use all your skills and capabilities. They may be as simple as being able to make someone feel comfortable in your presence, smiling at everyone you meet or being an expert on a particular topic. Your skills may seem insignificant because they feel so familiar to you, but we all have them.

To create your own success strategy take yourself back to a moment in time when you decided to do the thing that has proved your greatest success in life to date. Then cast your mind back and write down every step you took along the route. Think about what led you to decide to take that action.

It may have been a simple thought, such as enough is enough, I have to do this, I want to do this, it is time to do this. It could be as simple as joining a slimming club, changing your job, moving house, or leaving a relationship. Go back to that thought and write it down.

What was your goal? After that initial thought you knew exactly what you wanted and you were determined to achieve it. It could have been that you no longer fitted into your favourite clothes, but it was enough to drive you forward. What was your strategy that got you motivated and helped you achieve what you wanted? That personal strategy is nearly always the same and it can be used for all your goals in life.

Now that you have found your hidden talents and skills, next you need to survive the danger zone. As soon as we decide to make a change in our life, the voice of self-doubt starts to creep in; a wickedly strong voice which is very good at giving you reasons not to take action towards what you want to achieve. Therefore, it is important to take action quickly and not allow this voice of doubt to creep in. Once you start listening to your negative thoughts they will kill your intentions. It is vital that you tune in, hear them loud and banish them.

Negative thoughts normally start with, "I can't" as in, "I can't spare the time" or "I am not" as in, "I am not qualified." Ask yourself what you avoid by holding on to these self-doubts. For example, "Why do I avoid changing my job or why do I avoid taking responsibility for my life?"

Consider what it will cost you if you remain in your comfort zone. Will you get the peace of mind and calm you are looking for or the partner to share your life with? You may avoid discomfort as a result, but the cost of holding onto your complaints will result in you losing any chance of getting your true desires.

Courage and willpower are essential attributes in order to achieve your goals, but you can do it. Keep your eye on your desired outcome, continue reminding yourself what your dream is, use all the tools you have and then success will be yours.

Getting what you want is a journey and who you become on the way is just as important as what you get at the destination. You will cause yourself a great deal of frustration if you forget to enjoy the here and the now, so remember to appreciate what you already have and use that as a tool to create happiness on a daily basis.

Step Into Action – create your own success strategy

🍵 Do the exercise given to you in the text above, in your journal

☕ Know what you want and your objective—write this down in your journal.

☕ Do research if necessary.

☕ Keep doing whatever it takes to get the result that you want.

☕ Take time to achieve your goal and make sure you also have time for yourself.

☕ Stay focused on the outcome.

☕ Change any behaviour that might stop you from achieving what you want.

☕ Make sure you are getting what you really want.

☕ Ask for help if you need it.

☕ Book a life coach if you are struggling to discover the steps to take.

Love yourself, you're worth it.

Having Self-Respect

"Never violate the sacredness of your individual self-respect."

~Theodore Parker

The inspiration for this chapter came from the movie Fearless. After a young Chinese boy is beaten up in a fight, he resolves to become strong so everyone will fear and respect him. His mother tries to explain that fear and respect are two very different things. She tells him, wisely, that in order to respect yourself, you must first learn to respect others. This theme of respect runs strongly throughout the movie and it is a theme that should also feature strongly in our lives.

Our own self-respect or feeling of self-worth is closely tied to our ego. In holistic terms, our ego is firmly linked to the solar plexus chakra. It is no wonder then that many of us find it difficult to separate the concept of "commanding respect" from that of "earning respect?" As our ego comes into play, there is a tendency to dominate and rule over others. As we plump our own feathers and tell ourselves how important we are, we generate an aura around ourselves that says, "Challenge me if you dare, respect me and have no fear."

This can be effective. The human psyche is very powerful and every event occurs twice, first in your head and then in reality. So by telling yourself that you are respected you will generate an air of importance, which others will notice. They will see this as evidence, in their minds, that you are someone who must be respected. This, in turn, will feed your own notion of self-importance. However, respect generated in this way is more aligned to fear than respect, which are two very different things. Respect gained in this manner is extremely hollow.

Similarly, those who make themselves totally subservient to others in order to gain favour or respect are equally unlikely to find what they are looking for. What respect would you have for someone who has no opinion of his or her own? Someone whose only beliefs are those you espouse? Someone who will never point out the error of your ways, even though they are plain for all to see?

Those who operate in this way have misguidedly given up all self-respect in the hope of gaining acceptance. Not only have they lost their self-respect, they are unlikely ever to gain the respect of those around them.

The key to finding self-respect is balance. We must find a way to recognise our own self-worth in an honest, positive, non-confrontational manner, whilst recognising the skills, competencies and attributes of others.

We must not be afraid to recognise and acknowledge the things we are good at, such as physical skills and attributes ("I am an excellent tennis player"), emotional skills ("I am a very good listener"), numerical skills ("I can do long division in my head") or even "whole life" attributes ("I am generally a good, honest, caring person"). These feelings of confidence, achievement and ability are essential feeds into our self-esteem, a significant part of our self-respect.

The danger arises when we stop making factual statements and replace them with those of a bragging or confrontational nature ("I am a much better footballer/

dancer/singer/worker/tennis player than you," or "I am a much better person than you") for example. As soon as we begin to measure our success or self-worth against the successes and failures of other people, we have begun, unwittingly, to erode our own self-respect.

Instead of measuring ourselves against others, we must learn to see, accept and appreciate the skills, attributes, strengths and weaknesses of others, in isolation from our own feelings of self-worth. Learning to recognise, accept and appreciate others for who they are will help to generate feelings of self-respect in them as at the same time as encouraging them to respect you.

There are seven basic human rights. These are simple rights to which we are all entitled:

- The right to be here, to exist.
- The right to feel and express needs.
- The right to act, be innovative, free,
- The right to love and be loved.
- The right to speak and hear the truth.
- The right to see.
- The right to know the truth.

Understanding and remembering that you have these entitlements will help to prevent your self-esteem and self-respect from being taken away. However, it is equally important to remember that everyone else is just as entitled to these rights. By actively granting these rights to everyone you meet, you will demonstrate your respect for them. And in doing so, you will not only generate respect from them, but also build your own sense of self-respect.

I have noticed in my therapy practice that when one of these rights is violated or taken away from you, or you are violating or taking it away from another, all sorts of problems occur within the health and psyche of both parties. Self-respect and respect of others is vital for a healthy and happy life. It is a good idea to remind yourself we are all totally linked in some way.

At the end of the day, it is very simple:

You must respect yourself or others will not respect you.

In order to respect yourself, you must first learn to respect others

Hold these thoughts in mind with everyone you meet over the next few days and see how your self-respect, your respect for others and their respect for you, all grow.

Step Into Action

☕ Remember and understand that "commanding" respect is not the same as earning respect! Commanding respect implies fear.

☕ Do not let the ego take over and the human right of being innovative and free.

☕ You must respect yourself or others will not respect you.

☕ If you let others treat you as a door mat, or if you are always subservient, how can you expect others to respect you?

☕ In order to respect yourself, you must first learn to respect others.

☕ Remember the seven Basic Human rights and that you and everyone else are entitled to them.

☕ Do not measure your success or self-worth against the successes and failures of other people.

♨ Instead of measuring yourself against others, learn to see, accept and appreciate the skills, attributes, strengths and weaknesses of others.

Respect yourself, you're worth it!

Self-Belief: The Power of Me

"God didn't have time to make a nobody, only a somebody."
~Mary Kay Ash

A re you? Might you be? Could you be? I might be. I would like to be. I could be. I should be. I will be. I am.

Which of those statements conveys the strongest feeling? Might you be a beautiful person? Would you like to be a beautiful person? Could you be a beautiful person? Should you be a beautiful person? Will you be a beautiful person?

How about if you stand up, look in the mirror and say, "I *am* a beautiful person?" How much stronger does that statement sound than all the other statements above put together? Why is this so? Because it is definitive; no ifs, buts or maybes. 'I *am*', period. The statement conveys total self-belief. When you say the words "I am" the words and energy that follow summons creation with a mighty force.

If you really believe you are going to succeed, there is a very good chance you will. Sadly, the inverse is also true; if you believe you are going to fail, you probably will.

As we go through life, the stories we tell ourselves shape our lives in dramatic ways. If we tell ourselves we are strong, capable, beautiful people, we will develop an air of confidence around us. Others will notice this and conclude that we are strong, capable, beautiful people. We, in turn, will notice their reaction to us which will fuel our feelings of self-belief. In the same way, if we tell ourselves that we are weak, incapable and ugly, our self-belief will be fuelled with those negative thoughts. Our mind is a very powerful tool.

How many times have you said to yourself, "I would really love to but." Why not just say, "I am never going to try." It amounts to the same thing, your belief is that you can't. There is a reason (the but) which is stopping you and so because you believe you can't you won't. What if that was just a story? What if you changed the story and instead said, "I can and I will?" People often tell you to focus your energy into the positive, but the truth is that most of us simply focus all our energy into our beliefs. If we believe we can't we focus our energy into making sure we can't. If we believe we can, we focus our energy into making sure we do.

As Henry Ford said, "Whether you think you can or think you can't, either way you are right."

We all have self-belief, but many of our beliefs hold us back instead of moving us forward. We need to eliminate the negative beliefs and replace them with positive ones. Be the person you want to be instead of wanting to be that person.

In the movie Star Wars there is a wonderful scene where Yoda uses "the force" to lift Luke Skywalker's ship out of a pool of water. Totally amazed, Luke turns to Yoda and exclaims, "I don't believe it!"

"That," says Yoda, "is why you fail."

Here are some useful steps to bring some positive self-belief into your life:

Step Into Action

☕ Make a list of something you would like to be: Slim, a singer in a band, a nurse, a small business owner, a pilot, a managing director, whatever features strongly in your life.

☕ Stand in front of the mirror, look yourself in the eyes and say out loud, "I *am*........(slim, a singer, pilot, a managing director)"

☕ Say it again and again until you really feel it. Say it loud, say it proud and *believe* it!

☕ Repeat this every morning when you wake up and every evening before you go to sleep.

☕ Write it in your journal, post it on your screen saver, on your fridge, or anywhere you will frequently see it

☕ Notice how uncomfortable this feels at first, but how it gets easier every time, until you reach the point where you really do believe it. As this happens, notice how those around you seem to believe it too.

☕ Notice how things will start to change in your life; synchronicities that happen leading the way to your success.

☕ No more "buts," no more "tries" only "can do's!"

☕ You are now ready to repeat the process with the next self-limiting belief in your mind.

☕ Believe in you, because you can do anything you want to do. You are also perfect just as you are. The world or the Universe would not be whole or perfect without you and you can achieve anything you want. The Universe will conspire with you a long as you make the first move and you believe!

☕ Believe in yourself. Be the person you really are and fulfil your true potential.

You can achieve anything you want. You are a genius beyond description, so tell yourself that and become aware of who you really are.

Love yourself, you're worth it.

The Masks We Wear

*"We understand how dangerous a mask can be. We all
become what we pretend to be."*

~Patrick Rothfuss

Most of us live behind masks all the time based on the
false assumption that we are somehow safer behind
them. These "masks" are there because we have either not
figured out who we are, or because we're afraid that who
we are won't be accepted, We feel that people may not like
who we truly are so we attempt to become what we think
they want us to be. Or because at sometime in our past we
have been belittled, beaten, or even imprisoned for showing
who we were and our ideas and beliefs did not fit into main
stream society beliefs and values.

It is like a little child hiding behind his own hand and
actually believing that his whole body has disappeared. Yet
as we all walk around trying to be 'normal,' we overlook one
extremely important factor, which is that other people are
looking at you as their 'normal' gauge, just as you're looking
at them for yours.

The person who is 'you' is exactly what you have
created 'you' to be. Your experiences and your beliefs, your
motivations and your actions have shaped you into who you
are. Yet when you hide behind a mask and try to act out of
alignment with who you really are, you will at some point
begin to feel uneasy and nothing will be quite right. When
you're afraid to be who you really are, you lose touch with

the truth and act in ways you may later regret. So why do so many of us feel uneasy speaking up for our beliefs and living our own lives while dreading the thought of not fitting in? Because we are afraid that somehow we are inferior to those around us and we lack the confidence to believe otherwise.

Yet if you really think about the worst thing that could happen if you feel free to be yourself, it is that someone may not accept you. It's really not so bad is it? After all, if you can't be genuine with someone, why do you want to be around them? If you can't be 'you' then what is the point of being anyone? We are all born as unique individuals with unique gifts to offer the world, only you are perfect as you are, only 'you' can be 'you' and we all individually fit into the universal jigsaw puzzle. We all have our place just as we truly are.

Masks come in many forms, such as a comedian, perfectionist, victim, know-it-all, peacemaker, wallflower, over achiever. Starting in adolescence, we learn to rely on superficial identities that define our place in the world. As we mature, our masks become more sophisticated and entrenched in our personalities.

A secret in life is that all people feel insecure. Masks are ineffective solutions to the problem of insecurity, either trying to fool others by pretending to be superior, egotist or a know it all, or sadly fooling yourself by acting inferior. Often people who hide behind 'I know better' masks are insecure in themselves and often also in denial about situations in their lives.

The masks we wear on Halloween, we can take off at the end of the evening. The personality masks that hide who we are become harder to take off as each year passes and we really begin to believe the web of lies that we have been spinning.

By wearing masks, we make our relationships safer and more predictable. We protect ourselves from rejection, presenting the "me" that others will embrace or accept, or which is socially acceptable. We don't want others to know the fears and insecurities and thoughts behind our mask/s and yet everyone else will have their own fears and insecurities too. Every person you meet will have some sort of fear or doubt or insecurity or something they wish to hide from or from you.

You might think that the commitment and intimacy of marriage or long term partnerships would make authentic communication easier. If you share a bathroom, bed and chequebook with someone, why hide behind a mask? Ironically, marriage and long lasting/life term partnerships is often where we become most guarded because no other relationship is potentially more hurtful. Although being betrayed by a friend or co-worker stings, the rejection of a spouse/lover is devastating. We cannot simply walk away from wounds inflicted in marriage or long term partnership or relationship. So we choose to stay safely behind masks rather than reveal our vulnerability. If you share a bathroom, bed and chequebook with someone, why hide behind a mask?

Our masks might be one of the greatest threats to intimacy in marriage and life partnerships. In fact, many people understand their spouses in terms of their masks, never considering what might lie beneath: 'Sam is a workaholic' 'Lucy is someone who can never say no.' 'Jane is the life of the party, but she's a grump once she gets home.' 'Never start an argument with Tom, he won't ever let it go.'

Knowing each other behind the masks, however, helps couples and friends understand why they respond the way they do. I have been privileged to sit in sessions/workshops/

seminars in which a husband and wife and long term partners have really seen each other for the first time. She sees his fear of failure behind his perfectionism. He sees how terrified she is to trust his leadership because of the ways her father abused his authority, for example.

Another time the man owned up to seeing and knowing there are other beings out in the Universe and astral projection and his partner also knew the same and had phychic gifts of clairvoyance but neither had said anything because they didn't want the other to think they were mad, or indeed spying on the other.

In another session, the husband who very clearly loved his wife, said he would love to see her just once without makeup on….in the 28 years they had known each other and throughout a marriage of 27 years, his wife had never once let him see her without her makeup on. She slept in it, she locked herself in the bathroom when she was showering and cleansing it off and re-polishing it. She had not let him be there at the birth of their son because the doctors had insisted she take off her makeup. She thought and really believed she was ugly without it and she only ever wanted to be beautiful for him, the love of her life! How very sad! All because an old bitter aunt had once told her as a child that she was an ugly duckling and should never been seen without makeup on or she wouldn't get a husband!

In some ways, we are all scared little children in a grown-up world, afraid of failure and rejection. Our masks help us feel in control. The intimacy we desperately long for, however, can only be established once we reveal our vulnerability and it is a hard thing to show but a wonderful to do so as it gives us immense strength and personal power and inner peace.

If your fears and insecurities make it difficult for you to be who you are, you do need to release them if you can and maybe get help from a councilor or qualified therapist to do so, because when you let go of your need to be how others want you to be the sense of contradiction within you will disappear and you will then feel your inner confidence shining through.

Your best approach is to let go of wanting to be the way others want you to be so you can simply be yourself, realizing that your true self is far more beautiful than any mask, no matter how bejeweled it may be.

Step Into Action

Take off your own mask. The only mask you can take off is your own.

☕ Write down a list of what masks you wear in front of your spouse/lover/friends/work collegues and such like.

☕ Write down what vulnerable feelings or fears lie beneath?

☕ Start to look for ways to deal with any feelings or issues.

☕ Talk to a trained councilor, coach or therapist if you need help to deal with the issues.

☕ Learn to ask and listen. People love to talk about themselves. Even shy and reserved people will gladly unload their thoughts and feelings if you ask the right questions. Show them you genuinely want to know and their masks will fall away.

☕ Don't be afraid to be 'you.'

Love yourself, you're worth it.

Moving Forward

"You can't have a better tomorrow if you are thinking about yesterday all the time."
~Charles F Kettering

Many of us have great ideas, big dreams and exciting goals for the future, but likewise many of us also feel stuck and unmotivated. We dream but never act! As I listen and observe, in my work and to people in general, I have noticed a few themes as to what prevents us from moving forward.

Generally speaking, what we need to do most to get unstuck is the opposite of what the majority of us actually do. You need to stop beating yourself up and give yourself a break. Does that sound familiar to you? How many of you beat yourselves up when you just cannot seem to sort things out?

This means you need to be kind to yourself in spite of your frustration. It means accepting your feelings of hopelessness so you stop using so much precious energy trying to push these feelings away. Getting unstuck means embracing the whole you, the you with the good intentions, the you who takes action now and again, the you who keeps tripping yourself up.

The message is simple: do not beat yourself up as this only keeps you stuck where you are! Does that make sense? Of course it does!

How do we get unstuck and start moving forward?

You first have to start believing in yourself and take your personal power back. One of the biggest mistakes we make when we feel stuck is telling ourselves that it is due to outside circumstances, such as a lack of money, too many problems or the influence of other people. All of us face challenges from time to time as this is a natural part of life. We just need to remember that we have choices and this gives us power to move. They may be tough choices, like selling a home to relieve financial pressure or walking away from an abusive relationship to reclaim our self-esteem, or even from your place of work as the energy and stress of it is just too much for you to handle. Do not mistake tough choices with having no choices at all. We always have choices. How we deal with those choices is what makes or breaks us.

We often find comfort in a place of helplessness because it provides an excuse for why things are the way they are, almost like a comfort zone, but it gives us victim mentality. However, holding this position or mental attitude will ultimately be what takes you down. To turn this habit or tendency around, stop and consider one area of your life you really want to change then ask yourself the following question: "What choices do I have in this situation?" Pick one and do something about it. There is always a choice!

The next thing you need to do is manage and change your mindset. Feeling stuck is always fuelled by our state of mind, which means the thoughts we think from moment to moment. When we feel unmotivated, it is because we are thinking predominately negative thoughts. When we feel trapped, it is because we constantly tell ourselves that there are no options. When we feel hopeless there is a good chance that the thoughts running through our mind are something like this: "Why bother?" or "It's not possible" or "I should just give up."

The key to turning this self-defeating, victim mentality habit around is to take control of your thoughts. You can use this simple technique:

For one week, make yourself your own mantra and repeat the phrase "I can do anything!" or "Everything I want is possible." Say this with real belief and conviction throughout the day.

Whether or not you believe it or whether it seems rational or irrational is irrelevant; do it anyway. Say it to yourself when you first wake up, repeat it in your mind while you brush your teeth, sing it while driving to work or while you get the kids ready for school. Repeat it to yourself all day at work, right up until you go to sleep. Continue telling yourself and notice how your mood and perspective shifts.

Take note in your journal and see how your mindset changes and how the feelings deep inside shift.

Remember, when you always do what you have always done, you will always get what you always got! So make the change and start right now! Become unstuck and move forward. You can do it! Everyone can do it! Take action now!

Keep good company and positive people around you. Every successful person I have ever met, spent time with or read about has emphasised the importance of having highly motivated and positive people around them. So surround yourself with motivated people who are just as committed as you. Those who do not give up at the first hurdle, but pick themselves up, dust themselves off and start again. Do not surround yourself with negative, self-destructive, jealous or just plain boring and lazy people. Find the motivated ones, stick with them, learn from them. Think outside the box, believe in yourself and move forward.

Step Into Action

When feeling stuck and unmotivated do not blame outside circumstances and do not think like a victim.

Remember we always have choices.

Turn your mindset around, make yourself a personal mantra, along the lines of, "I can do it" or "everything I want is possible."

Use this mantra everyday all day for a week or more.

Make notes in your journal of how your mind and feelings shift in energy as you do this.

Surround yourself only with positive and motivated people, learn from them.

Think outside the box.

Believe in yourself and do not give up at the first hurdle.

Decide which area of your life you are most stuck in and then make the changes that need to be done. Change your thoughts around the situation.

Remember that to move forward you have to take action now!

Love yourself, you're worth it.

Be the Change
You Want to Be

"When we are no longer able to change a situation...we are challenged to change ourselves."
~Viktor Frankl

The only thing constant in this world is change...or is it?

We all want change. We have great ideas, big dreams and exciting goals for the future. Yet, while many of us talk about change and our desire or need for it, many people go no further than that.

If this sounds familiar, do not worry, as you are not alone. Psychologists have spent many years studying what seems to be a natural resistance to change, even when we initiate the change ourselves.

Change, by its very nature, means moving out of your comfort zone into new, unmapped territory. You think you know what the terrain is like on the other side, but you have never been there so you are not totally sure. It can be a little scary taking that first step. But that is all that is needed. One step in the right direction will lead you on your path to change and help you tear yourself away from the imaginary glue that has been sticking you where you are.

Nevertheless, this is easier said than done. Whether in personal or business life, most people can clearly articulate any number of reasons why they cannot take that first step.

Others might see them as excuses, but to you they are hard and fast reasons. If you put enough energy into giving life to these reasons, they will hold you where you are forever. However, if you were to put the same amount of energy into beating down these reasons, you would soon find yourself on the way to a new you.

A good friend and associate, Adrian Gilpin, talks about this on his Inspired Self course. He uses the example of an elastic band. If you stretch an elastic band in front of you, you will feel the tension (or energy) trying to pull your hands back together. If you let go of the end of the band it will immediately snap across to the other hand as the stored energy is released. Strangely enough, no matter which end you let go of, the result is the same, the band immediately snaps across to the other hand.

Now, imagine that one hand is where you are today (the here and now) and the other hand is the future (where you want to be). If you simply let go of the here and now, the tension between where you are and where you want to be will shoot you towards where you want to be. Of course you could just as easily let go of where you want to be to ensure that you remain firmly rooted in the here and now.

The first step towards making positive changes in your life is to take back your own personal power. Our place of power always lies in the recognition that we have choices. All of us face real-life challenges, but we always have a choice. Exercise your right to choose and choose to move forward. Put your energy into making positive choices and positive outcomes rather than negative ones. You will soon discover that it takes no more effort to move forward than it did to stick to your comfortable little rut!

Having taken back your personal power, having made

some positive choices and having channelled your energy into creating positive outcomes, you are now ready to master the second step towards positive life change; managing your mind and thoughts. Feeling stuck is nothing more than a state of mind. When we feel unmotivated, lethargic or overwhelmed it is because we are thinking unmotivated thoughts. When we feel trapped it is because we consistently tell ourselves there are no options. So the key to turning this self-defeating habit around is to take control of your thoughts. Take the word "can't" out of your vocabulary and replace it with "can." Keep telling yourself, "I can do anything" and notice how your mood and perspective shifts. As it does so, tell yourself positive stories. When you think about your future, think only the most positive outcomes. When you daydream about getting promoted, do not dwell on the challenges that lie between where you are today and the future you want to create. Instead, go straight to that future and dream about how wonderful your life is there. Do not imagine that it could be so, imagine it *is* so and before long you will begin to believe it is so. Then others around you will also begin to believe it, which will encourage you even further.

And remember, Rome was not built in a day nor will you change your life overnight. Be patient, be passionate and persevere. In the words of Lao-tzu, "A journey of a thousand miles begins with a single step."

Step Into Action

Here are a few ways that you can take your first step into change:

☕ Choose one area of your life that you would like to change then in your journal identify three choices you have available to you at this time and write them down. If you cannot come up with any, ask a friend or someone you trust for help.

☕ Create a new screensaver that flashes and moves the words "I can do anything!" across your laptop screen, or phone screen. If you do not know how to do this then your first active step can be requesting help from someone who knows how.

☕ Pick up the phone and schedule lunch, dinner, tea or a telephone conversation with a highly motivated friend who will support you quest for positive change. Ask him or her to help you create a simple action plan.

☕ Book a coaching session with a professional life or business coach to help you through any blocks you may have on your journey to change.

☕ Join an evening class or workshop to help you learn something new to help you on your journey forward and step into the positive changes.

Love yourself, you're worth it.

Being True to Yourself

"A bird doesn't sing because it has an answer, it sings because it has a song."

~Maya Angelou

Over the years of practising complimentary therapies, being a life and business coach, holding regular workshops and listening to people's problems, I have learnt quite a lot about what makes life great and the things that get in the way of success. People tend to grow up, get married, have children and along the way they lose their identities. They do what society expects them to do rather than what they really want to do. Some of the things I have learned may be useful to anyone who is about to undergo a major change or who is contemplating a major change.

☕ Follow your heart. Pay far more attention to what *you* think than what everyone else thinks. The most important relationship you will ever have is with yourself. One of the biggest regrets I often hear is the regret of listening to everyone else except for the self. So start making your own rules and follow them. At the end of your life, the most important person you will have to please is you.

☕ Spend more time on the who than the what. What you do will always be less important than the person you become. Knowledge is wonderful, but it will never take you as far as your courage, your integrity and your reputation. As you go through life, you will face various challenges and obstacles as life is not always an easy path. When you do, perhaps ask yourself similar questions to these:

How can I grow from this experience and challenge?

What lesson can or do I need to learn from it?

How can I use this challenge to make me a better person?

☕ Be willing to bend the rules. Learn how to disappoint others in a kind and gracious way. Get comfortable with people not liking you. Understand and accept that not everyone will like you, just as you will not like everyone. Always aim to be an original thinker and do not be afraid of conforming to others expectations of what they think you should be or do. Allow yourself to be the individual spirit that you were meant to be.

When I was growing up, people used to think I was a little strange so I hid my abilities and tried to conform and be "normal." It was not until I started to accept that we are all different and unique and that we all have individual gifts to offer that I slowly started to become me. I still struggle with confidence, but I am getting better all the time because over the recent years I have been pushed outside of my comfort zone and so have done things I would never have thought possible.

Your willingness to rock the boat will set you apart from 95 percent of the people you meet throughout your life. It can be very tough at times and far easier to back down and conform, but it is important to do what you are here to do. It takes courage, but you will always be happier for it. Nothing can ever stay the same, things change all the time, so be part of those changes and new ideas. Be the instigator of breaking down barriers and bringing out new ideas and concepts and do not quit when things get hard and frustrating. Keep believing.

☕ Start practicing or doing one small thing a day or week that frightens you. It could be something like asking someone on a date, going for that promotion, learning to dance, ski or sing, or changing your hairstyle. Small acts of courage strengthen your ability to take even bigger steps later, like deciding to write your own book, recording your first CD or running the marathon. Courage builds confidence and confident people rarely settle for less!

☕ When you are excited about doing something or trying to make an important decision, turn to people who will encourage you to take a chance; ones who believe in you rather than those who tell you why something will not work. Surround yourself with positive people who challenge you to reach beyond your fear rather than play it safe. There will always be people telling you why an idea is risky or why you cannot do something. That advice is usually based on the mistakes they have made or the chances they did not take because they were afraid. Always remember this, "someone else's past does not equal your future." Stick with positive people who believe in you and encourage you.

☕ Stay connected with those you love and those who

love you. Pick up the phone and call a friend or visit a loved one rather than send an email or text message. When we reach the end of our lives, it is who we loved and who loved us that matters the most. Make time for those you love and those who love you. Emailing or text messaging are valuable tools for staying in touch with people but real life connection is far more important and makes people feel much happier and cared for.

☕ Remember, your life is a canvas and you are the artist. You alone are responsible for your life and the picture you paint. If you remember that, your life will quite literally become a work of art, with all the colours and textures that you choose yourself.

☕ Also remember, "Where there's a will there's a way." Do not give up when things get hard and do not ever let anyone or anything put restraints or shackles on you. Do not give up when your heart tells you something is right, no matter what others say. Hold that dream/ vision in focus, believe it and it will eventually come to fruition.

Step Into Action

☕ In your journal write down things from your past that gave you a positive outlook on life including events and people who helped you build your self-esteem.

☕ Write down any empowering labels that others gave you.

☕ In times of success and joy what did you learn about yourself? How can you use those feelings and those lessons in your life now?

☕ What things do you like about yourself now? Are

you happy, positive, friendly, helpful, energetic?

☕ Think of some positive metaphors to describe you, for example, a shining light, an earth angel, as energetic as the wind, a rock of strength...

☕ What descriptions do you not like about yourself? How can you change these or let them go?

☕ Are you painting your true canvas of your life and how you really think and who you really are?

☕ What labels, roles and descriptions would support you as you create the future and the life you want?

Love yourself, you're worth it!

Daring to Dream

*"Dare to live the life you have dreamed for yourself. Go
forward and make your dreams come true."*
~Ralph Waldo Emerson

Most of us have dreams or have held dreams. Some of us
do realise those dreams, however many of us do not,
as life somehow gets in the way, social conditioning stops us
or we simply do not believe our dreams can come true.

Recently, a group of friends sat together and the
conversation turned to dreams. We decided to share our
dreams with each other. One friend's dream was to sing in
front of a full audience at the Albert Hall in London. Another
friend, who makes beautiful jewellery, said she wanted to see
her designs being worn on the cat walks in Paris.

Another friend wants to obtain a private pilot's licence
and fly around the world at his own pace. My dream is to
stand in front of an audience of thousands and share stories
of angels and crystals and how people can discover the innate
magic in them to shift their lives. I also dream of writing a
successful book, such as this very one you are reading!

While sharing our dreams, we also talked about the
messages we received about having dreams as we grew up.
There were a mixture of parents, adults without children,
singles and teenagers at the table and we learned a lot from
each other. Some of the things we spoke about were very
eye-opening and thought-provoking.

It seems that if your parents never learned (or allowed

themselves) to dream, there's a good chance that your ability to dream has been suppressed in some way. Many parents were raised during a time when dreams were considered a waste of time, a set-up for frustration and disappointment. As a result, the implied rules were "be happy with what you have," or "don't have high expectations." Some were told that dreams are not for "the likes of people like us," they are only for the rich.

I found one particular dream very sad. One lady said it was her dream to one day be "happy." As a child, she had been told that happiness was an illusion and she has no memory of ever being truly happy.

Personally, I was always told to come back from "cloud cuckoo land" or to "get real." If I did dream, I would automatically think it would not happen so I stopped. I am still paying the consequences of those put me downs, although I am slowly starting to believe my dreams and can come true. Now they are coming true, but it has taken 52 years to get there! However it is never too late to dream to have our dreams come true.

During the conversation several teenagers asked, "Can dreams really come true?" My answer was, "Yes, so long as you believe and continue believing." I wish I had been given that advice as a child. Another person revealed that he was taught that dreams rarely come true so he did not even bother to have them. How sad.

I once read the following statement, "Make sure your dreams are inspired by your heart, not your history." I only truly understood what that meant when a friend once said that early in her career she realised she was pursuing her father's dream of building a business, rather than her own dream. She admitted that her work often felt frustrating and stifling and she had to work hard to stay motivated. It is important to make sure that your dreams reflect your true aspirations rather than those of someone else.

Another great lesson I learnt was from a teenager. When I asked her to share her advice on fulfilling dreams, she said, "You need to keep at it. If you don't do something every day to further your dream, you'll lose momentum and eventually it will wither away and die."

While the idea of fulfilling a dream may seem impractical or silly, experience has taught me that our secret dreams often reflect the very thing we have come here to do. So, if that's true and I believe it is then the question is: "What dream or fantasy do you need to start making a reality so you can say, 'That was the perfect ending to a beautiful dream?'"

To help you figure it out, here are some steps to help you.

Step Into Action

 Use your journal to write down your answers and once you have an answer do not get caught up in A to Z thinking. Focus on the next step, the one you need to take to make it real.

 What is your greatest dream or fantasy?

 What would you do? Who would you be with? What dream would you fulfil?

 Once you have an idea, write it down, it is possible that you already know the answer.

 Remember no dream is silly or stupid and we all have the right to dream what we wish.

 What does this dream or fantasy say about you?

 What parts of your dream or fantasy need to be

incorporated into your present life?

🍵 How do you feel when you consider pursuing it? Does it feel impossible or achievable?

🍵 Is it your dream or does it belong to someone else?

🍵 Don't be afraid to dream and pursue your dreams. Sometimes the idea may seem frightening or silly. But it is your dream and if you don't follow it now in this life when do you expect to?

🍵 Dream big, dream anything you wish and then make it real.

Love yourself, you're worth it.

Understanding Your Path in Life

"Life is a great and wondrous mystery and the only thing we know that we have for sure is what is right here and right now. Don't miss it."

~Leo Buscaglia

One of the biggest challenges we face is remembering that life is a journey. If you focus only on the destination you will not enjoy the milestones along the way. We all have our own unique abilities and energy, our own strengths and purpose for being here on earth. Every choice we make is an opportunity to find fulfilment and to grow and to be true to our self. Instead of living a hectic, rushed and unconnected life, take time and enjoy the journey, enjoy your time here and all that life offers for you never know when this particular lifetime will end.

We tend to get so wrapped up in our lives that we often forget what we are doing, which makes things complicated. Life is often demanding and uncertain. However, sometimes our trials and tribulations are just what we need to make us think about our life path. Just because things are confusing or challenging now, it does not mean the road ahead will always be like that. Many of us choose to take the hard roads, perhaps because we like to believe that the greater the struggle, the greater the victory. Or because we are taught from an early age that life is not easy. We often make life far more complicated than it should be, but life is not meant to be a struggle.

It is said that each of us has a purpose, something we are to do in this lifetime. The problem with this is that we then tend to think we are here to achieve one great thing and that is all. We stress ourselves out searching for what it is and then our judgement is clouded and we feel we are heading in the wrong direction or getting nowhere. To me life is like a collection of thoughts, feelings, desires and experiences, which gives us the freedom to change our path and life as we want and therefore able to really enjoy it.

We most likely do have something we are here to achieve, but how we get there is up to us. There are times when we are so far off track that the Universe throws something our way in order to get our attention. In the end this helps us get back on track toward doing what we came here for. This has happened to me several times, along with many people I know. Think of all the people who have had near death experiences, overcome severe illness or survived horrifying accidents, only to come out the other end totally unscathed but completely changed. This is an example of a wakeup call! These people radically change their lives and suddenly they live rather than simply exist and they are an inspiration to everyone they meet.

In order to understand your life path, it is essential to understand where you are now and how you got here. By looking back at your life so far with an open and unbiased mind, you will notice how your life has evolved and how you have got to where you are now. By reflecting on the days gone by, our minds and spirits remember the things that worked for us, along with those things that did not. However, remember that the past is gone and we cannot bring it back nor can we remain living in it. Trying to do this only causes anguish and sorrow and then nothing will change. Learn the lessons, accept them and use them to help you move on.

Sometimes, we get to do what we want to do and we get the things we want to have. Other times we simply do what we have to, but all of it is connected to the choices we have made. Nobody's destiny is left strictly to fate and it never leaves you. It is you that leaves it when you get stuck in a rut and live with a set of false and self-limiting beliefs refusing to listen to your inner self. Your life path is very unique, just as everyone else is unique to their own life. Take the time to ask yourself what you really want out of life and then think how you can make it happen.

Because the majority of us are much more familiar with the things we do not want, a simple place to start is to start by making a list of what you *do* want and focus on that. Sometimes a little reverse-engineering can lead to amazing discovery. In order to find your true path, you must learn or accept what is true to you. So stop thinking about what you do not want and instead concentrate on what you do want then start changing your life so that it is more fulfilling.

Some paths are smooth while others have numerous bumps. Life, with its twisting turns, its pain and sorrow, its fun and laughter, causes us to grow. Some days, the only way to know where we are going is to pause and acknowledge how far we have already come. When it comes to your dreams, always believe they are reachable. Own your dreams whether they are big or small. Enjoy the little successes as much as the large ones and that way all of them will be just as gratifying as the final outcome.

Be flexible about the time it takes to reach your goals

and dreams. In the words of John Lennon 'Life is what happens when you are busy making other plans.' If you cannot manage to attend any classes or all your plans and activities in one week do not give up or convince yourself that you do not have the time or ability. Resume them as soon as you are able to do so. Stops and starts are a part of life, so turn dreaming into doing. It is far easier than you think.

Whether you know where you are going or you have only just figured out where you have been there is still uncharted territory left for you to explore. Do not fear whatever comes next because fear can keep you still. Chase your dreams, plan to fulfil your desires, follow your heart and honour the person you have become. The next step in your life is what you have decided it will be. Remember, life may be a journey, but you are in the driver's seat! You own the canvas to your life and you paint it with the colours and textures you want.

Face each day with an open heart and mind and work as hard as you play!

Step Into Action

☕ Think about all the good things that have come your way this year and in years past. Write them down in your journal and keep adding to them. This creates positive energy.

☕ Acknowledging and being grateful for your blessings creates and sends a great vibrational energy to the Universe that returns even more blessings to you. So write them down in your journal too.

☕ Remember, whatever you focus on, whether it is fear

and lack or love and prosperity, is what manifests in your life. So think only positive thoughts. Focus only on what you want!

☕ You do not have to deny your struggles, but keep your mental and emotional focus on what is right about your life, not on the struggles.

☕ Analyse where your life may be out of balance. Are you caring for others, but not taking time for yourself? Are you eating, drinking or spending too much? Are you working hard and not playing enough?

☕ Are you spending all your time on meaningless activities while trying to find a job?

☕ Are you too busy for your spiritual life?

☕ Take time out to connect with nature. A walk in the park, the forest or the beach will bring you that connection. It will also help to clear some of the clutter in your mind.

☕ When you have analysed your life you can start putting it into order and remove or change anything that is holding you back.

☕ Create a "vision" of how you want your life to look.

☕ Book a life coaching session if you still have difficulties in finding balance and your way in life.

☕ Stop making excuses and start to live your life now.

Love yourself, you're worth it.

Achieving Your Potential

"Focus on the journey, not the destination. Joy is found not in finishing an activity but in doing it."

~Greg Anderson

I am sure most of you reading this have dreams for the future, of reaching your desires and achieving your full potential, but you are stuck or do not know how to start achieving it.

There is an old joke (it may not be that funny but it is relevant to most of us at sometime or other) about a couple driving round the countryside looking for a village, who find themselves totally lost. When they stop to ask a local for directions he says, "Oh well, if I was trying to get there I certainly wouldn't start from here."

Most of us go through life trying to improve ourselves; to be the best we can and to fulfil our destiny. Some of us are more successful at this than others and when faced with failure, most of us review what we have done so far in order to identify what we did wrong and then we try again and again and again. But maybe we are not doing anything wrong along the way. Maybe we are simply not starting from the right place.

Consider a pizza maker. He takes the ingredients to make the pizza dough and the ingredients to put as the toppings and then he makes them into pizzas. With time and effort and practise he will improve his skill and his ability and will make all kinds of different flavoured pizzas. They may become thicker or thinner, smaller or bigger and made to order from many people of many different tastes and requirements. There is, however, a limit to his skill. At the end of the day they are just pizzas. But who said he has to be a pizza maker? Who said he can only work with pizza dough and ingredients.

Instead of trying to simply do a better job of what you already do, why not turn the process on its head? We all have a unique set of gifts and talents, the key is to discover them and in doing so discover your unique purpose in life. Having discovered your true purpose, focus your mind and all of your energy on achieving your purpose. So how do we do this?

In order to train your mind, look into the centre of a flower or candle flame and concentrate on nothing but what you see in front of you. At first, your mind will wander. As it does so, catch your thoughts and bring them back to the flower or candle flame. Look deep inside the image in front of you and focus. With a little practice, you will soon learn to focus your mind on a single thought. You can now begin to visualise your future. It is essential to understand where you are going so you know when you have arrived.

Visualising is an important part of this process and also "feeling" what it will feel like when you have achieved it.

Set aside ten minutes each day to take stock of where you are and what have you achieved. Are you on track? What else do you need to do? Praise yourself for each step you take towards your vision, but do not fret over "failures." See everything as nothing more than an experience; a lesson you can learn from or even as a different way of doing something.

As you learn your lessons and put your positive thoughts into action, you will be amazed at the results. Perhaps you will discover that you do not want to be a lawyer or movie star after all. Perhaps you really want to be a writer, or a gardener. Maybe you will discover a whole new set of skills which will give you the happiness and fulfilment you have been looking for. If nothing else, perhaps you will at least feel a little happier.

In the words of Robin Sharma, author of *The Monk Who Sold His Ferrari*, "The secret of happiness is simple. Find out what you truly love doing and then direct all of your energy towards doing it. Once you do this, abundance flows into your life and all your desires are filled with ease and grace."

As you visualise your future begin to create a plan to achieve it and then you will believe in yourself and your own uniqueness and know that anything is possible.

Step Into Action

🍵 Set some goals, make them achievable and realistic. These will alert your mind to the positive thoughts to focus on along the way.

🍵 Write them down and read them often, maybe put them in your journal and also put them on your fridge, mirror, computer screen, or somewhere you see frequently.

🍵 Examine yourself. What are you good at? You can ask a trusted friend to help you with this if you don't know or believe you are.

🍵 What really makes you happy?

🍵 What skills and attributes do you need to become

the person you want to be and achieve that future?

☕ What skills and attributes do you already have?

☕ Set timelines to achieve your goals and tell the people around you. This creates positive pressure and encourages you to stay on the path and achieve your goals.

☕ However, do not beat yourself up if you don't always make the timeline to your goal. Just set yourself another timeline.

☕ Stay focused on the future. Do not worry about the past failures or things you cannot change. Focus only on your goals and the things you can change.

☕ Give yourself praise when you have achieved something towards that future.

☕ Make yourself a vision board and pin pictures and words on it relating to the future you want to create.

☕ Take action starting today! It is easy to start visualising and feeling the future you want.

Love yourself, you're worth it.

The Magic of a
Stick-to-it Attitude

"Choosing a goal and sticking to it changes everything."
~Scott Reed

Over the years I have had many opportunities to learn about the value of developing a "stick-to-it" attitude when it comes to doing things important to the nourishment of my body, mind and soul. Even when things have got really tough and I have just wanted to give up, I have seen the difference it makes to hang in there and keep going.

What about you? Do you tend to quit when things get hard, frustrating or boring? Or do you have a "stick-to-it" attitude that encourages you to keep plodding along even when things are tough?

Developing the ability to hang in there when things get hard or when you feel tempted to quit, is the difference between living a mediocre life or an exciting one that reflects your soul's deepest longings and desires. It is about training yourself to work through the temptation to quit on those things that you know in your heart and soul really matter.

If you tend to look for shortcuts when you know you need to stay strong, do not worry. With a little patience and practice, you can teach yourself to develop a "stick-to-it" attitude. All it takes is awareness as you approach everyday tasks in a new way. For example, the next time you decide to de-clutter a room, make sure you actually finish the project.

When you are tempted to leave a few items in a corner, tell yourself, "No, I've got a stick-to-it policy," and then stick to it. When clearing out your wardrobe, do not stop or hang onto things because they may fit you when you have lost a few pounds or because you may need that T-shirt to go to the gym, when you never go. Clear your wardrobe out and do not stop until the task is completed. While weeding your garden, do not give up on the last two feet. Hang in there and pull those last few weeds out. When your cheque book does not balance and you are tempted to let it go until next month, challenge yourself to keep looking until you get it right.

Stop yourself the moment you start to rationalise why you deserve to make a purchase on your credit/charge card that you know you cannot pay off. Take the tough road, say "No!" and stick to it. When vacuuming your car, pick up the mats and clean underneath rather than do a quick surface cleaning. If you decide to get fit, do not go to the gym once, feel good about it and then never go again. Set yourself a realistic fitness target and keep going on a regular basis until you reach your goals.

As you review the above keep in mind that the point is less about the actual activity and more about installing a new behaviour pattern that will make a difference in the quality of your life.

My determination to carry on when it all seemed too much gave me self-respect, trust and a feeling of satisfaction, knowing I have the inner strength to move mountains if I have to. It also helped my self-confidence. If you step into the challenge of your 'stick-to-it policy' you will start to feel much better about yourself.

After reading this chapter there is a good chance that

you will catch yourself right in the middle of walking away from something you do not want to deal with. Stop and think for a moment then do whatever it is you are putting off. Cook that healthy meal rather than grabbing a quick, unhealthy snack. Or finish paying all your bills rather than leaving a couple for later. You will be glad you did as you walk away with the strength and peace of mind that comes from a job well done.

Step Into Action

♨ In your journal make a list of some things that you really need to do, for example, clearing out your closet, losing weight, balancing your cheque book, tidying up the garage.

♨ Next decide which one you need to do first, then make a "stick to it attitude."

♨ If you are going to clear your wardrobe, give yourself plenty of time to do it. Then be determined to start and finish it. Do not walk away when there are just a few items left to decide upon. Stick to it and finish it.

♨ Clutter left in your closet stays as clutter in your mind when you know it needs finishing, so "stick to it."

♨ Cook that healthy meal you know you need instead of grabbing a pizza or an unhealthy snack.

♨ You have lost 5 kilos in weight and you have three more to go, "stick to it" and do not give up. Know you will feel so much better and the confidence of the achievement will make you feel so much better.

♨ Pat yourself on the back and enjoy the feeling of fulfilment in your accomplishments of finishing what you started no matter how tough it was.

☕ Make the "stick to it attitude" a policy. It will soon become a natural way of life and will fill you with peace of mind when you know everything that needs to be done is done.

Love yourself, you're worth it.

Nurturing the Energy of the Soul

"There is undisturbed peace deep within you, feel it, express it and put its powerful profound energy to use."
~Ralph Marston

As we grow on our spiritual path, we develop our inner knowingness, a sense of self-worth and who we really are. During this process a statement we often ponder is, "we are not our bodies, we are only our soul, our body is just the house or the shell that protects it this lifetime" If this is true, you could be forgiven for asking yourself "so, what is the body for?"

One way of thinking about the body is that it is the vehicle which carries our soul along the highway of life. It allows us to exist on this earth and to learn new lessons. It is the physical manifestation of our soul, our energy, our being. It allows us to do good things for the world and those around us, as well as for ourselves, which is our real purpose for being here.

We live through our physical bodies, but often we neglect our physical selves. This can lead to emotional and physical issues, but more importantly, in forgetting to nurture our physical selves we forget to nurture our soul, leading to even deeper spiritual issues. Nurturing ourselves is the only way we can nurture our soul.

Beyond ourselves, we are all here to help and be of

service to others, but we need to nurture our own souls first in order to nurture others. Your physical body is a temporary structure which will last you for this lifetime only, yet most of us pay an excessive amount of attention to our appearance. We obsess over our reflection in the mirror, we worry about what we look like, we worry about what other people think. It is very hard to remember that inside we are far more than the flesh and blood that surrounds our bones. What really matters is the soul within.

As we grow spiritually, we realise that our soul needs to be nourished, nurtured, loved and given the same level of care and attention as our physical body. But how do we do that? How does one feed a soul? Your soul is really not very demanding. All it desires is a little love and energy. The simplest way to achieve a harmonious, open, well-fed soul is to systematically treat it with love and care.

"Feeding your soul" or "nurturing your soul" means doing something just for you—something that gives you a feeling of accomplishment or something positive to look forward to. It is not just for relaxation; it is for your spiritual growth.

There are many ways you can create a sanctuary and a loving space for your soul, such as meditating daily. This is one of the easiest things to do, but people are often turned off by the word "meditate" and they avoid sitting in quiet contemplation. There is nothing difficult in meditation. You can make it as hard or as easy as you wish. To meditate you can lie or sit down and listen to beautiful music, sit outside in nature and listen to the sounds or sit by the beach and watch the waves crashing. Creating a sanctuary for your soul requires spending time alone, being quiet and relaxing, connecting with your own essence. Regardless of how you do it, the most important thing is that you do. When you are quiet and still you allow the voice of your true self to speak to you and then you can listen to it.

Only when we find the quietness in our own minds can we then begin to hear our inner teacher, our soul and only then we may receive some intuition. Only when you are ready to recognise and value the wisdom that you carry at the core of your being will you turn your attention inwards.

It is important to quiet the chatter of your mind in order to make room for the voice inside to speak to you. It may even give you an answer to your questions and prayers. That little voice could be your intuition nagging you to make a different choice in your life. It is through quiet and solitude that the truth speaks the loudest.

By creating a sanctuary for your soul to relax, you will recharge your battery. Like a car running out of fuel, it is the same with your body and mind. When you start running out of energy, you become short-tempered, irritable, impatient, tired, spacey and you often become ill. You start to live your life by accident rather than on purpose. So many people go through the motions of life, rather than truly live it.

Take time to listen to your intuition with patience and things will start to become clear, including the reason why you are here, who you really are and what you have to give. Then you can begin to live your life "with purpose." When we start to live with purpose, each day we wake up energised and in tune with our soul.

From today why not practice taking a few minutes for yourself each morning. Even just sitting with your morning cup of tea or coffee in your garden, or at the window or even in the bathroom. Feel the peace and collect your thoughts and just really be in the moment. You never know when the

Universe is going to put someone in your path whose life you can help to improve even if just giving them a smile.

Step Into Action

Everyone needs time for reflection. I am sure you are familiar with the saying, "I can't even hear myself think?" Maybe it has been a long time since you truly listened or took time out for yourself so start practicing today.

☕At some point today sit down, be quiet and listen in. You might be surprised at what you hear. Then do it again tomorrow.

☕All you need to do is remember that you are the listener and not the noise.

☕Play your day back before you go to bed. What was so great about your day? What would you have done differently?

☕Find time to sit in quiet contemplation each day even if only for 10 minutes so you can sort out your thoughts.

☕Perhaps you want to plan your day or think about a decision you need to make.

☕Make some time each day to do something for yourself, to nurture yourself and your soul. It may be sitting still for two minutes to listen to a favourite song, to watch the sunset, to lie in a warm bath of bubbles or to walk in the garden.

☕Taking this time for reflection allows us to grow, express gratitude, be organised, value thoughtfulness and nurture our souls.

Love yourself, you're worth it.

Conclusion

Look inside and touch your essence

*"The human soul is God's treasury, out of which he coins
unspeakable riches."*
~Henry Ward Beecher

Throughout the book, at the end of each chapter you
have found words of encouragement, to love yourself
and that you are worth it.

You are made up of two aspects. The first and most
obvious being the psychological self with all that it entails.
It is your personality, which is made up of your thought
and emotional patterns, your past experience, your dreams
and desires. Your personality is lovable with all its strengths
and weakness. You are unique and perfect just as you are.
Imagine that you are a saint who does everything right: your
partner would divorce you instantly, your friends would
probably avoid you and you would probably not feel as if
you fit in anywhere.

The second and less readily accessible aspect is your soul
or your essence. This essence is subtle and can be found only
in silence and in the absence of mental/emotional activity. It
requires no change, no improvement and no action on your
part. All that is needed is for you to begin paying attention
to this small delightful flame within that gives each and every
moment a blessed atmosphere. When you become aware of

this all of your suffering ends. This is the place where you can go daily and where you will find peace. It is perfect and no one can take it from you; only you can deny it or lock it away. It is your soul and your connection to all that is, has been and ever will be. It resides deep within your core centre. It is tender and it needs nurturing just as you do.

When you go within you touch the stillness and the pure love that lies at the core of your being.

We all have eyes and ears, we all live in the outside world and we all tend to look outwards for what we want or to fill the empty spaces and feelings, as that's where everything seems to be happening and where it superficially appears that we can find what we need. So why would we look inwards? It is simple. Because the magic we seek and the love, beauty, peace, truth, happiness is inside, not outside. We already have what we are searching for. We so often forget to look inwards, beyond the materialistic world and shallow memories of recent experiences. As a result we never see our own true self and the treasures hidden inside. We become strangers to our soul to our real self or core essence and we suffer.

Right now you can take a few moments to stop, to just 'be' and to look inside and see. Don't rush, don't search, don't be hard on yourself, just look, feel and be aware.

When we find the quietness in our own minds and start to look inside we begin to feel the flame of love, peace, serenity and our connectedness to all that is. We then connect to who we are. It is only when we are ready to see and acknowledge the value of the wisdom and love that we carry at the core of our being that we will turn our attention inwards and 'listen in'. As you have this book, you have all the tools and maybe you are now ready.

You know there is nothing to fear, that there is only love and your essence is love, peace and radiant light. Become the beacon of light and love that you are.

A little practice and patience will be needed. Today, be quiet and listen in. You might be surprised at what you hear, see or feel. Then do it again tomorrow and the day after and every day beyond this day.

To do this you only need to remember that you are the listener and not the noise, that your essence is love and light, that you are reaching into and nurturing your soul, your essence, fuelling the flame of love and peace. You will no longer be a stranger to your soul. You can do it, as everyone can do it! Remove your mind from everything and everyone, go beyond the cares and the troubles of the world and become detached from all that is not inside.

You will then be free to radiate light, to feel the flame of love that burns so brightly in your soul, to go beyond time and space, to feel the peace and to no longer be a stranger to yourself.

Step into action

☕ Take time to 'be' by sitting in stillness, or quietness for a few minutes each day.

☕ Find the time to meditate daily, even a few minutes a day, perhaps just before bed, when you first wake up, or when drinking your morning tea or coffee. Meditation is the process of getting to know yourself completely, both who you are inside and how you react to what is outside.

☕ Through meditation, you will discover a very different "you" from the perhaps stressed, spiritually lost, sad or troubled person who may seem superficially to be "you." You will start to realise and recognise that your true nature, the real you, is actually very loving and always positive. You will begin to discover the love and peace right on your doorstep, you will no longer be a stranger to your real self, which in turn will connect you to the very essence of love and all that is. Find the peace inside and then the outside will become peaceful too and your suffering will end.

☕ Meditation isn't hard, it is simplicity itself. It helps you to reconnect with your soul, your essence. There are many different ways to meditate but they all bring you to your real self. The easiest way is to sit with yourself, in quiet detachment from the endless chatter in your mind and just 'be.' You can keep your eyes open or closed. Personally I feel that closing your eyes is best, but others like to keep them open...find your way! Meditation is for everyone, there is no magical way of doing it. Some like to make it ritualistic and difficult, others prefer simplicity, like myself. Even watching nature, looking up at the vastness of the sky, watching the clouds float by or the stars at night, watching the birds, hugging trees and prayer are all forms of meditation, as they bring you to a central place of calm and peace and then you start to become aware of your essence and beyond.

☕ Every day on the wings of your thoughts let there be only love, compassion and peace and then you will radiate your bliss and your light outwards to the world.

Love yourself. You are love. Your very essence is love!

Closing thoughts

Now that you have read *Comfy Slippers and a Cup of Tea* I hope you are more in touch with your own wisdom. We already know all of the answers, however unfortunately they have been buried deep within our subconscious as we have evolved and developed as human beings. It is up to us, as individuals, to take the steps towards remembering once again.

May you find the confidence to walk through the world in peace, prosperity, love and joy…

About Julie Lomas

Julie has a diverse background and runs a successful business called Conscious Connections, based in Bahrain. It is a company dedicated to bringing healing and personal fulfilment into all areas of society and into the mainstream business world. As a certified life and business coach and inspirational speaker she addresses areas such as personal confidence, self-esteem and stress management. For many years Julie worked in the fast moving, highly competitive and stressful airline industry, therefore she understands the high pressure corporate world and how the health of the people involved and their families are affected.

She is also a practitioner of and teaches holistic complimentary therapies, energy awareness and spiritual development. She has always been in tune with the energies around us and she has successfully been able to incorporate spirituality and business ethics into her teaching methods.

Very fortunate to have extensively travelled and to have had the opportunity to live around the world, including the Far East, Middle East, Australia and the Caribbean, she has been exposed to the spiritual ways, beliefs and cultures of many people. This is incorporated into her teachings, writing and work.

Her journey into the complementary, holistic medicine and therapies world started after an illness in her early thirties. Becoming disillusioned with conventional medicine and its sometimes unpleasant side effects, she eventually discovered Homeopathy, Reiki, Crystals and several other therapies, which helped her on the road to recovery.

This led her to start to learn about herself and others and open up to the world of spiritual development. Training extensively in holistic therapies, including the original Japanese method of Reiki, (Jikiden Reiki) crystal and colour therapies amongst other diverse holistic therapies, she finally became a Certified Life and Business coach, enabling her to treat the person as a 'whole' (holistically).

As a child Julie had always been able to see and feel the energies around her and she had a very deep sense of 'knowing.' She would regularly have chats with the energies she saw or sensed and spent a great deal of time outside conversing with nature and the universal energy. However, she soon learnt not to say much to the adults or other children as it was dismissed as silly, weird or a vivid imagination. As a result, Julie closed herself off to it.

However, as she trained, she once again opened herself up to the world around her. That is when her abilities to 'see' 'sense' and 'feel' returned and once again she felt truly connected to all things.

This is now what Julie encourages us all to do; to tap into the universal energies that are there to help us and always will be. It is nothing to be worried or sceptical about. Everyone is able to do this, as it is part of our makeup.

Julie helps you to understand yourself better and to understand the connection between your mind, body and spirit by using the energies and tools around us and our deep innate knowing that we can all heal ourselves.

Julie and her husband, Roy, currently live between Spain and Bahrain, a small but beautiful desert island country, which inspires her work and where her company and main practice is based. She travels worldwide teaching and facilitating workshops about holistic/complimentary therapies, stress management and personal self-development.

Recommended Reading

Unstoppable, Adrian Gilpin

This is Reiki, Frank Arjava Petter

Being in Love, Osho

You Can Heal Your Life, Louise Hay

Celestine Prophecy, James Redfield

Excuse Me Your Life is Waiting, Lynn Grabhorn

Chicken Soup For the Soul, Jack Canfield

The Seven Spiritual Laws of Success, Deepak Chopra

How To See Yourself As You Really Are, The Dalai Lama

The Seat of the Soul, Gary Zukav

The Light: A Book of Wisdom, Keidi Keating

The Four Agreements, Don Miguel Ruiz

Conversations with God, Neale Donald Walsch

Happy for no Reason, Marci Shimoff

The Passion Test, Janet Attwood

The Power of Now, Eckhart Tolle

Appendix

Reiki. The Japanese art of Reiki was discovered by Dr. Mikao Usui in 1922 when on a meditation and fasting retreat on Mount Kurama in Kyoto. Since then, Reiki has spread all over the world, giving joy and happiness to millions of people from all races, religions and social backgrounds. It is a hands-on natural healing therapy. Reiki is the life-force inherent in all beings, sentient and insentient. It permeates everyone and everything, therefore anyone can learn Reiki and how to direct energy consciously.

Reiki is naturally emitted from the physical body of all beings. Learning Reiki first and foremost makes you aware of the energy flow and enables you to direct energy at will. There are five basic principles to learning and incorporating Reiki into your life, which enables you to live a healthier, happier, calmer and peaceful life.

www.reikidharma.com
www.jikidenreiki.com

Lightning Source UK Ltd.
Milton Keynes UK
UKOW06f2325110516

274082UK00015B/367/P